RUNNING FORM

HOW TO RUN FASTER AND PREVENT INJURY

Owen Anderson, PhD

HUMAN KINETICS

Library of Congress Cataloging-in-Publication Data

Names: Anderson, Owen, 1947– author.
Title: Running form : how to run faster and prevent injury / Owen Anderson, PhD.
Description: Champaign, Illinois : Human Kinetics, [2018] | Includes bibliographical references and index. |
Description based on print version record and CIP data provided by publisher.
Identifiers: LCCN 2017024200 (print) | LCCN 2017031218 (ebook) | ISBN 9781492551409 (ebook) |
    ISBN 9781492510383 (print)
Subjects: LCSH: Running—Training. | Physical fitness.
Classification: LCC GV1061 (ebook) | LCC GV1061 .A54 2018 (print) | DDC 796.42—dc23
LC record available at https://lccn.loc.gov/2017024200

ISBN: 978-1-4925-1038-3 (print)

The web addresses cited in this text were current as of October 2017, unless otherwise noted.

Acquisitions Editors: Tom Heine, Michelle Maloney
Developmental Editor: Anne Hall
Managing Editor: Caitlin Husted
Copyeditor: Jackie Gibson
Indexer: Nancy Ball
Permissions Manager: Martha Gullo
Graphic Designers: Joe Buck, Julie L. Denzer, Angela K. Snyder
Cover Designer: Keri Evans
Photograph (cover): Getty Images/AFP/Fabrice Caffrini
Photographs (interior): Jason Allen, unless otherwise noted
Photo Asset Manager: Laura Fitch
Visual Production Assistant: Joyce Brumfield
Photo Production Manager: Jason Allen
Senior Art Manager: Kelly Hendren
Illustrations: © Human Kinetics
Printer: Versa Press

We thank the Okemos High School in Okemos, Michigan for assistance in providing the location for the photo shoot for this book.

Human Kinetics books are available at special discounts for bulk purchase. Special editions or book excerpts can also be created to specification. For details, contact the Special Sales Manager at Human Kinetics.

Printed in the United States of America

10 9 8 7 6 5 4 3 2 1

The paper in this book is certified under a sustainable forestry program.

Human Kinetics
P.O. Box 5076
Champaign, IL 61825-5076
Website: www.HumanKinetics.com

In the United States, e-mail info@hkusa.com or call 800-747-4457.
In Canada, e-mail info@hkcanada.com.
In Europe, e-mail hk@hkeurope.com.

For information about Human Kinetics' coverage in other areas of the world,
please visit our website: **www.HumanKinetics.com**

E6558

RUNNING FORM

HOW TO RUN FASTER AND PREVENT INJURY

Contents

Acknowledgments

I owe a debt of gratitude to a large number of very special people who have assisted with the creation of this book.

Without the assistance of my great friend and colleague Walt Reynolds, this book would never have been possible. Almost every week for over two years, Walt and I discussed running form in great detail over lunches of raw fish, miso soup, noodles, and scalding-hot green tea. It was Walt who introduced me to the unique form terminology used in this volume, including the all-important SAT (shank angle at touchdown), MSA (maximal shank angle), ROS (reversal of swing), FAT (foot angle at touchdown), and the incredibly important golden ratio (ROS/MSA), which determines which runners will be found on the podium at the ends of elite competitions or—in the case of non-elite running—which runners are most likely to be injured as they pursue their running goals. It was Walt who made the amazing discovery that, with just one exception, world-record holders at distances ranging from 100 meters to the marathon all shared a common SAT. Walt found that Usain Bolt (world-record holder for 100 meters) and Dennis Kimetto (world-record holder for the marathon) land on the ground with their legs in very similar positions, leading to the discovery that there is an optimal way of striking the ground. Walt also created an important new definition of running economy: *the velocity a runner can attain in relation to the impact forces he creates with the ground*. Walt is currently coaching Mark Otieno, a sprinter who holds the Kenyan records for 100 and 200 meters. I consider Walt the most knowledgeable running form expert in the world, and you will find his concepts and recommendations throughout this book.

I am also indebted to the elite Kenyan distance runners I am currently coaching and managing, who utilized both the video-form analysis described in this book and also the recommended form drills to improve their performances significantly. Cynthia Limo (silver medalist in the 2016 IAAF World Half Marathon Championship and first-ranked road racer in the world as ranked by ARRS in 2016), Mary Wacera (world silver and bronze medalist in the 2014 and 2016 IAAF World Half Marathon Championships), Monicah Ngige (two-time winner of the Cooper River Bridge Run 10K and champion of the 2017 Monterey Bay Half Marathon), Mary Wangui (victor at the 2017 Tulsa Run 15K), Iveen Chepkemoi (first in the 2017 AK Sotik Cross Country meeting in Kenya), and Gladys Kipsoi (winner of the 2017 Pittsburgh Half Marathon) all employed the techniques described in this book to improve their performances and decrease their risk of injury.

A number of sub-elite runners I am currently coaching were also instrumental in improving the book. Dr. Larry Kurz, Rabbi Lawrence Kelemen, Yaakov Nourollah, Dr. David Rosmarin, Charlie Morrow, Meir Kaniel, Paul Gray, Rabbi Elie Karfunkel, Rifky Karfunkel, Yisroel Gelber, Yosef Weissman, and Omeed Hakimi have all utilized the techniques described in this book to run faster while keeping the injury bug at bay. I owe an extra-special debt to Larry Kurz, Rabbi Kelemen, and Yaakov Nourollah for their incredible faith, friendship, and unending support.

I am also extremely grateful to my editors at Human Kinetics. Anne Hall, Caitlin Husted, Michelle Maloney, and Tom Heine worked tirelessly to bring this book to fruition and have provided perfect guidance and assistance. They were patient and supportive always, even when the time devoted to coaching and managing my elite team resulted in long writing droughts. My editors' vast skills at improving the writing found in this volume and at pairing text with essential photos, figures, and illustrations have improved this book immeasurably.

I have also been helped enormously by the research carried out by other scientists. Notably, the investigations conducted by Peter Weyand at the Locomotor Performance Lab at Southern Methodist University, Daniel Lieberman of the Department of Human Evolutionary Biology at Harvard University, and Irene Davis at the Harvard Medical School and the Spaulding National Running Center have provided key insights concerning vertical and horizontal propulsive forces during gait, the effects of running form on impact and propulsive forces, and the interactions between various aspects of running form and both performance and the risk of injury.

Introduction: The Importance of Form

The inspiration for this book came on a January evening when I visited the track at Kezar Stadium in San Francisco with my friend, Hans Overturf. Hans announced earlier in the day that we would go to Kezar for his weekly speed workout.

It was a Tuesday evening, so it was not surprising that Hans was going to conduct his speed training. After all, almost every runner seems to believe that an up-to-date running program must include speed work on Tuesdays. What *was* astonishing was that there were more than 300 runners on the track that night—a real shock to a man who had just arrived in the Bay Area from Lansing, Michigan. Back home, I would have been lucky to find one hardy soul, draped in at least seven layers of wind-resistant material, shivering and sliding along the Lansing River Trail in a desperate attempt at a workout.

The throng at Kezar had no such difficulty with the weather (it was a balmy 57 degrees at the track), and the exercisers were quite diverse, as I had come to expect in San Francisco: There was a nun walking the track in her habit, a businessman jogging the oval in his suit and tie, an elderly man in bedroom slippers, a gray-haired woman pushing a walker, as well as an array of runners of all ages and ability levels, including some highly fit participants from several area running clubs.

The eye-opening and highly disturbing shock of the night was the realization that almost all the runners were moving around the track with terrible running form. The slowest runners had bad form, but so did the fastest harriers. Their gait patterns were quite similar, despite the wide range of speeds. Men and women were infected with serious cases of horrible running form.

And yet nothing was being done about it! Coaches ringed the track like ants at a picnic, calling out splits and instructions to the runners as they passed by. Among the coaching cohort, there was careful attention to stop watches and ample information provided about overall workout composition, work-interval lengths, recovery times, numbers of repetitions, running velocities, availability of sports drinks, and so on. But not one peep emerged about how the runners were actually moving.

I noticed one runner in particular who obviously had a well-trained machine—the heart and leg muscles that drive his running. This individual was traveling around the track at a strong pace and with great and unyielding stamina. But he was hitting the ground on each step with an absolutely straight leg and with a high-impact strike directly on the heel, which was, of course, making contact with terra firma far out ahead of the runner's center of mass. It seemed to me that any casual observer should notice the massive braking action and lofty impact forces in play on each and every one of his collisions with the earth. And yet his coach called out "Great job, Joe!" (The runner's name has been changed to protect his guilt.)

Another runner was landing in a slightly less leg-destructive way, but I could easily see that she was setting her foot onto the ground ahead of her body, adjusting, modulating, checking, and stabilizing the foot, and then finally using active contractions of her core and nonsupport thigh to swing her leg and body over the support foot and prepare for the next landing. It was as though she were pole vaulting over each leg, bringing her body from far back and expending great energy to get her mass over the forward leg. There was little hint of the springiness that is a natural feature of the human leg in optimal action. Rather, each step involved hard work—demanding, oxygen-consuming effort—that was eating away at the runner's economy. Furthermore, the runner was spending most of her time stuck to the ground instead of flying forward.

Observing the scene, I felt more than a little sick. The runners clearly didn't know what to do. Many were outstandingly fit (if one thinks of fitness as a parameter that resides solely in a runner's machine). They were able to complete amazing quantities of work. The members of one club were even conducting a 20-by-400-meter interval workout. And yet, it was as though the runners were moving along with humming, powerful Rolls-Royce engines in vehicles outfitted with stone, square wheels. There was great power locked in the runners' cardiovascular and muscular systems; yet there were huge, performance-limiting forces at work in the ways in which the runners' legs and feet interacted with the ground.

As a coach, I strongly felt that the coaches present at Kezar were betraying their runners. After all, there *is* a right form for running, and one of a running coach's tasks is to teach that optimal form to all of his or her athletes. It seemed as though the coaches had thrown their runners out on the track and asked them to do incredible things without providing them with the skills needed to run correctly.

That was hurtful to me because running with bad form is not a trivial matter. Poor form obviously hurts performance (both during competitions and workouts), but it also wrecks running economy and increases the risk of injury, making it much less likely that a runner will be able to train consistently and improve.

It was also hurtful because it is so easy to learn proper running form. Little equipment is required, and a runner can transform his manner of running quite progressively and significantly, as long as the correct drills and techniques are employed in training. The Kezar Stadium runners could have been moving faster and with less effort—if only they had possessed the knowledge necessary to throw away their square wheels and replace them with Michelins.

Strangely enough, running is one of the very few human activities in which one's innate way of doing things is viewed as being naturally optimal and therefore not subject to change. In other athletic pursuits, we learn how to swim, to hit a backhand in tennis, and to snap off a curveball. But when it comes to running, we are allowed to do whatever we want. The implied belief is that each person runs in an optimal way, even though her gait may be strikingly different from a top performer or a runner with excellent economy. Although it is not often stated, the accepted belief is that each runner moves in a way that is shaped by her unique anatomy and physiology, and therefore her form should not be tampered with in any significant way. By some sort of magic, each runner's brain is supposed to know exactly how to produce a gait pattern that will lead to the fastest possible 5K or marathon, the lowest risk of injury, and the most enhanced economy of movement.

One reason that poor form is so widespread is that science has generally done a very bad job of demonstrating that form can be corrected and of providing runners and coaches with practical, easy-to-use, and correct advice about form. For example, in a classic study carried out at Wake Forest University several years ago, runners were advised to make a number of changes to their form, including the use of a heel-striking landing pattern, slight trunk flexion throughout gait, increased knee flexion during stance, and a conscious attempt to take longer strides [1]. Despite the use of positive verbal and visual feedback provided to the runners over the course of five weeks of training, the "upgraded" running styles did not lead to improvements in economy or decreases in perceived effort while running. In fact, there were no positive changes at all associated with the form alterations.

The results of this research are not really surprising. Although heel-striking is the most popular method of hitting the ground while running, and has been widely accepted as a key component of good form for decades, a heel-strike strategy magnifies both braking and impact forces (as will be explained in this book) and therefore is unlikely to be associated with enhanced economy. Increasing stride length artificially is also not likely to be linked with better economy, as other studies have shown [2]. And increased knee flexion when the foot is on the ground may serve only to elongate the stance phase of running and thus reduce stride rate and increase the relative proportion of time during which a runner is glued to the ground instead of flying forward. This is an important distinction, as we will see later in this book. Overall, the Wake Forest research was flawed because it did not identify optimal running form end points.

Fortunately, a reasonable body of scientific research—including the work of Daniel Lieberman at Harvard University (3)—exists to guide us in our pursuit of optimal running form. Also, a massive amount of experience gained by the author while working with runners of all ability levels, from elite to novice, has proved to be extremely useful for providing form guidelines.

These guidelines do far more than help runners look smoother and better as they run. When a runner moves along with proper form, he is faster and more economical, and his risk of injury is significantly lower. It is my sincere hope that the contents of this book will help you make great improvements in form and will thus lead to the attainment of even the loftiest of running goals and to a far more satisfying and productive overall running experience.

Content Overview

This book is arranged in the following way: Chapter 1 introduces you to traditional views of running form and outlines the deficiencies in conventional concepts of form. Chapter 2 then takes a look at the form utilized by the vast majority of runners and discusses differences in form between elite and non-elite runners, identifying form factors that help elites produce superior performances.

Chapter 3 then takes you on an exciting trip into the elements of form, pinpointing those aspects of form that are critical for your success as a runner. (Success is always defined in this book as the achievement of your goals as a runner in an injury-free fashion, not as the establishment of a world-class performance time.)

Chapter 4 explains how good running form can enhance your performance and decrease your risk of injury, and then Chapter 5 takes you into the world of assessing and measuring your running form in a productive and beneficial way. You will learn that you can evaluate your form optimally with an app and an easily downloaded runner's metronome for your smartphone.

You will then be off and running and ready to learn the drills that optimize your running form. Chapter 6 shows you how to develop a perfect foot-strike pattern that puts more spring in your step and decreases the rate at which impact shock passes through your leg. Chapter 7 teaches you how to optimize one of the most critical factors of form: the angle of your shank at the moment your foot hits the ground. This angle determines the braking (and breaking) forces associated with every step you take as you run and the amount of propulsive force you apply to the ground—as well as the timing of that force.

Chapter 8 then teaches you to shorten your stance time, spending less time on the ground per step and thus advancing your cadence (the number of steps you take per minute as you run), which is a critical form variable.

Chapter 9 then helps you develop a slight forward lean as you run. This lean comes from the ankles, not from the hips, and helps you spring aggressively, upward and forward, with each contact that you make with the ground.

Chapter 10 then addresses the important topic of overall posture as you run. Chapter 11—a critically important section of the book—reveals how to put it all together, incorporating the various aspects of form into the best possible way of moving over the ground.

Chapter 12 contains an essential topic for runners: running shoes and their effects on both running form and injury risk. You will learn many things about conventional running shoes—including the pernicious effect they have on running form—and you will become a much wiser shopper when it is time to purchase a new pair of training or racing shoes.

Chapter 13 takes a look at form considerations for special groups of runners, comparing female form with male form and also examining what happens to form as a runner ages—and what can be done to keep aging from harming form. Chapter 14 teaches you how to use running-specific strength training to advance your form.

Chapter 15 closes this volume by showing you how to coordinate the drills and methods of form training with your overall training program so that you can optimize your running fitness while simultaneously optimizing your form.

Who This Book Is For

This book is intended for all runners: elite and non-elite, male and female, young and old, experienced and inexperienced. This book proves useful for runners who have suffered from injuries, because the techniques described in the book help protect against a wide array of running injuries. It is also for runners who want to get faster and for those who simply want to train more consistently and improve body composition.

The book has been written with the distance runner in mind, but—somewhat surprisingly—the sprinter will also find valuable information in the chapters. As it turns out, there are many similarities in form between distance athletes and sprint athletes. Both groups, if they are training properly, are trying to optimize a key form variable called the golden ratio (a variable you will learn about in chapter 3).

References

1. S.P. Messier and J.J. Cirillo, "Effects of a Verbal and Visual Feedback System on Running Technique, Perceived Exertion, and Running Economy in Female Novice Runners," *Medicine and Science in Sports and Exercise* 21, no. 2 (1989), S80.

2. "Effect of Stride Length Variation on Oxygen Uptake During Level and Positive Grade Treadmill Running," *Medicine and Science in Sports and Exercise* 18, no. 2 (1986).

3. D.E. Lieberman et al, "Foot Strike Patterns and Collision Forces in Habitually Barefoot Versus Shod Runners," *Nature* 463, no. 7280 (2010), 531–535.

PART

I

Why Form
Matters

Traditional Views on Form

It's personal. At least that's how running form has traditionally been viewed. Aiming for perfection of movement, swimmers practice their strokes, budding tennis players spend hours developing proper footwork and swing mechanics, and golfers constantly strive to optimize form, but runners usually, well, just run. It is commonly believed that running is such a basic activity that no instruction manual is required. But runners tend to run the way they breathe—with little thought about, planning for, or practice of coordinating gait. According to popular belief, each runner optimizes his form naturally as he trains, and the gait pattern that evolves is a function of the runner's unique anatomical and neuromuscular characteristics. Copying another runner's form or—dare we say it?—actually *learning* how to run from a coach or textbook is viewed as a dangerous enterprise, since it might violate one's own functionality and even produce physical injury.

Such popular and widespread views are illogical and run counter to experience. After all, running consists of repeated movements, motions that are replicated by all runners (1). When running speed increases, nearly all runners flex their legs more at the knee during the swing and sweep phase of gait (when a leg loses contact with the ground and swings forward and then backward prior to the next impact with *terra firma*) (figure 1.1*a*). Most runners decrease knee flexion during swing while running downhill and increase knee flexion when surging uphill. During swing, all runners activate their hamstrings to control forward movement of the legs. And as runners move along, each foot traces a kidney-shaped line of movement through the air and over the ground. This is called the "motion curve," or the path of the foot and leg during a stride (figure 1.1*b*).

The basic mechanics and neuromuscular patterns of running are not so unique after all, and it is highly questionable whether each runner develops her own optimal gait pattern. Except for walking, no other human activity is viewed as being optimally developed without instruction and learning, like in running. Skeptics may ask exactly what might be "optimized" when a runner develops his own style of running. It certainly can't be the prevention of damage to a runner's body, since up to 90 percent of runners are injured in an average year (2). Nor can it be economy of movement, since research reveals that certain types of training alter running form and consequently upgrade economy.

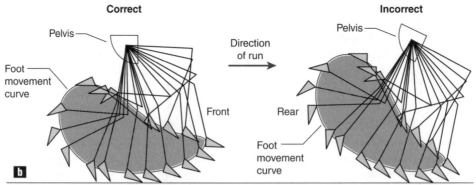

Figure 1.1   (*a*) As running speed increases, runners flex their legs more during the swing and sweep phases of gait. (*b*) A runner's foot follows a kidney bean-shaped line of movement through the air and over the ground.

Running on Square Wheels

An unfortunate consequence of this view—that every runner naturally optimizes his unique form—is that the majority of runners don't spend enough time trying to improve their form. After all, if form is already optimal, why should one attempt to change it? Serious runners tend to spend a lot of time devising challenging workouts in order to improve key performance variables such as $\dot{V}O_2max$, lactate threshold speed, fatigue resistance, and maximal running speed. However, they tend to ignore their own gait patterns and fail to develop strategies for upgrading gait quality. The frequent result is that such runners develop huge "machines"—voluminous hearts that can send large quantities of oxygen-rich blood to the leg muscles and responsive muscles with very high oxidative capacities. But these machines seldom produce the best possible performances, because they are hooked up to legs that fail to optimally interact with the ground (in other words, legs that operate with sub-optimal form). It is a bit like placing a magnificent Rolls-Royce engine in an automobile and then outfitting the vehicle with square, stone wheels.

Good-Looking Runners

Another traditional view suggests that how a runner looks while running is critical to form. Typically, tense, agonized expressions (a la Emil Zápotek, figure 1.2*a*) are discouraged, as are rolling movements of the head (a la Jim Ryan, figure 1.2*b*).

Figure 1.2 **Legendary athletes (*a*) Emil Zátopek and (*b*) Jim Ryun ran with seemingly non-optimal movements in their upper bodies, but did they really have bad form?**

Twists and turns of the upper body and excessive arm movements are generally frowned upon, as though upper body activity is the key determinant of proper form. According to popular wisdom, running should be a smooth and rhythmic activity, and good form should be free of bumps and jerks.

But shouldn't a definition of proper form go beyond smooth activity and control of the torso? Shouldn't it also include precise mention of how the feet, ankles, and legs are functioning, with actual scientific numbers placed on joint and leg angles, limb positions and movements, and foot angles at initial contact with the ground (instead of the usual reliance on vague pronouncements about high knees, soft knees, and springy ankles)? After all, forward propulsion is provided by the legs—not the upper body—and proper form should produce better, faster, more economical, and more injury-free movement. It is important to define exactly what the lower limbs should be doing (with real numbers, not just words), and this book will do just that.

Form and Running Economy

Traditionally, research into form has focused on economy of movement. Studies using animals reveal that they tend to move in ways that produce the smallest energy cost. At first glance, economy and form research using human runners also seems to support the "personal" view of running form (the notion that each individual develops the form that is right for him) because some studies have indeed suggested that runners naturally learn to optimize their stride length, a key component of running form. In one investigation, runners were found, on average, to naturally stride just one inch, or 2.5 centimeters, away from the stride length that produced the most economical running (3).

To understand such research, it is important to note that running economy is defined as the oxygen "cost" of running. If two runners are moving along at the same speed, the one who is using less oxygen (expressed per pound or kilogram of body weight per minute) is said to be more economical. Good economy is a predictor of performance and indicates that a runner can operate at a lower percentage of her aerobic maximum—and with lower perceived effort—at any velocity, compared with a runner who has poorer economy and similar aerobic capacity. Since the actions of the legs consume oxygen during running, it is logical to assume that enhanced economy is an essential goal of improving form. In other words, form transformations should be deliberately structured to optimize the actions of the legs and thus improve economy.

In another piece of research, running economy actually deteriorated whenever runners increased or decreased their stride lengths by relatively small amounts (4). So, is it possible that runners really do optimize stride length as a natural outcome of their training, without needing coaching around stride length? And if they optimize stride length, isn't it likely they also optimize other aspects of gait? Doesn't this mean that a runner should avoid tinkering with his own form, since what comes naturally is probably right for the body?

Simply put, no. These studies on stride length and economy have deep methodological flaws. When a runner changes her form, running economy associated with the new form can progress and improve gradually, over a period of several weeks. A snapshot taken immediately after form has changed will fail to reveal the ultimate impact of that change in form on the runner's economy. Therefore, research actually does not support the idea that runners optimize stride length, since the time periods involved in the investigations are too short. As a further rebuttal to the philosophy of "each-to-his-own" running, studies have shown that runners who make significant form changes can develop marked improvements in running economy (5).

Quantifying the Right Way to Run

Bear in mind that about 90 to 95 percent of runners are heel-strikers (6, 7), hitting the ground heel first as they run. As this book will demonstrate, heel-striking is not an optimal way to run, for a variety of different reasons, including the effects of such ground landings on performance and the risk of injury. There is a right way to run—a running blueprint applicable to almost all runners—and there is actually no reason to believe that optimization has occurred in each individual. Some runners do have great form, as we will see, while others fall far off the mark.

Numbers, Please

A key problem with traditional views on running form is that there has been nearly a complete lack of quantification of form. Traditionally, form recommendations have been made with the use of general statements, without identifying precisely how the body should be adjusted. For example, a runner may be told to maintain short, quick strides in order to have good form, without any specifications as to how short each step should actually be or how quick the cadence (number of steps per minute) should be. Nor is there usually any mention of exactly how a runner can progressively make the change from long, lethargic stepping to quicksilver cantering. Outstanding drills for developing great form have been in short supply (a shortage which will be remedied by this book).

As an example of the lack of form quantification, David E. Martin and Peter N. Coe, in their book *Training Distance Runners*, propose a number of elements of good form, including a head that is "well poised" and a trunk kept in a vertical position (8). According to Martin and Coe, the feet should be parallel to each other—pointing straight ahead during stance—and the arms should be held naturally, never hunched. The shoulders should be carried vertically above the hips, the elbows close to the body, and the hands loose and relaxed, with the fingers slightly bent. These statements are vague. Exactly how "poised" should the head be? And how exactly should the arms be positioned "naturally"? They also fail to quantify or even address the key components of form, which include joint angles of the feet and legs during various stages of gait. As pointed out by Walt Reynolds (9), running-specific strength training and running form guru, the following questions must be answered before form recommendations can be properly made:

- How should the foot strike the ground? Is a heel-, midfoot-, or forefoot-strike optimal?
- At first contact with the ground, where should the foot be in relation to the body's center of mass?
- What angle should the leg make with the ground at impact?
- What cadence is best?
- What is the optimal amount of swing and sweep during a gait cycle?

When runners attempt to develop better form by focusing on vague, non-quantified recommendations concerning the head, shoulders, arms, and hands, it is like cramming for a calculus test by practicing multiplication tables.

In their book *Bill Bowerman's High Performance Training for Track and Field*, coaches Bill Bowerman and Bill Freeman make traditional non-quantitative statements about form, calling for an "upright posture" while running, with the back perpendicular to the ground, a "tucked" pelvis, and little or no overall forward body lean (10). Bowerman and Freeman also recommend:

- Swinging the hands in an arc from the top of the hip to the center of the body;
- Utilizing a quick, light, and short stride with an effortless leg swing; and
- Choosing either a flat-footed (midfoot) or heel-to-ball landing, whichever is "most comfortable."

With such general recommendations, it could be difficult for a runner to determine exactly what optimal form is or understand how to create appropriate form drills and train in ways that produce great form.

Form Before Function

Hundreds of online articles provide form recommendations, often in contradictory ways and certainly without scientific backing for various claims. For example, an article published on the Runner's World website in 2014 advises that "it doesn't matter whether the heel or forefoot hits the ground first, as long as your foot is not in front of your knee" (11). The scientific or experiential basis for such recommendations is unknown, since research has shown that heel and forefoot-striking are associated with dramatically different impact forces as well as ankle and calf muscle workloads. It is also difficult to imagine a runner moving along while consciously keeping the feet under the knees at impact—and yet hitting the ground heel-first.

In the highly popular book *Daniels' Running Formula*, coaching legend Jack Daniels devotes approximately two pages total to technique or form (12).

In one section, titled "Foot Strike," Daniels writes that he sees little general advantage associated with the use of a midfoot-strike pattern, compared with a rear-foot landing, and vice versa. He suggests that if a runner used a heel-first landing, he should try to imagine that he is rolling over his foot as his body moves forward after landing (13). It is difficult to imagine what else a runner could do after striking the ground with the heel, since rolling backwards off the heel and springing forward off the heel are not desirable options. Daniels also advises runners to imagine they are running over a field of raw eggs as they move along, with the goal being not to crack any of the eggs (14). It is very hard to imagine how a runner could optimize propulsive force and maximal running velocity with such a strategy, especially since current research indicates that running speed is a direct function of vertical ground-reaction force; the greater the vertical force, the higher the running velocity (15). High vertical forces would crack a lot of raw eggs!

Correctly Identifying Elements of Good Form

The halls of academia have also largely failed to provide solid, practical form recommendations for runners and coaches. In a classic five-week study in 1989 (16), researchers at Wake Forest University used video and verbal feedback to guide a group of 11 runners through a variety of seemingly positive form changes, which included the following:

- Slight increases in stride length
- Small decreases in contact time
- Greater plantar flexion of the ankle at the end of stance
- Greater knee flexion during swing
- Higher knee flexion at impact with the ground
- Slight flexion of the trunk while moving forward
- Preservation of a 90-degree angle between forearms and upper arms during arm swing
- Heel-striking (instead of landing on the ground with the midfoot or forefoot)

At the end of five weeks, the Wake Forest harriers had not experienced even the slightest improvement in running economy. Five weeks should be a sufficient time for economy changes to occur, so what went wrong? It probably wasn't a great idea to advocate heel-striking, since there is little convincing evidence that heel-striking allows a runner to pound the ground toward better economy. But the main issue with this research is that it failed to help runners improve (or even identify) the key elements of form, including leg angle at the moment of contact with the ground, foot position and angle at ground contact, and *sweep* and *swing* of the leg during the overall gait cycle. Sweep is backward "pawing" action made by the lower leg immediately before the foot makes contact with the ground. Swing is the forward movement of the leg; it begins after toe-off and ends when the leg stops moving forward relative to the body—at the moment when sweep starts to occur.

That's not surprising. Traditionally there has been a systematic failure to identify the key elements of good form. As mentioned, form has often been viewed as an exercise in aesthetics, as though "looking good" is the primary desired outcome of form adjustments. People viewed famed runner Emil Zátopek as having terrible form because of his unusual upper body movements, but focusing on the upper body to assess form is comparable to having a physician check on your teeth to discover what is wrong with your feet. Zátopek's legs and feet interacted with the ground in very positive ways, but this has never been mentioned in the examination of his form.

The aesthetic analysis of form ignores the fact that form should be discussed in the context of function, running economy, risk of injury, and performance. The key elements of form must be the ways in which the legs, ankles, and feet interact with the ground. It is only via these interactions that propulsive forces are created and injury-inducing impact forces are handled and controlled by a runner's body. These interactions should be quantified and linked with optimal levels of performance, enhanced running economy, and the lowest possibilities of injury.

Runners vary quite widely in their form characteristics. A 1992 study, which examined several biomechanical variables in elite female distance runners of similar abilities, detected ample variations among the athletes (17). For example, "stance time," or the amount of time a foot spends on the ground as an individual runs, averaged 180 milliseconds in this group, but varied from as little as 167 to as many as 193 milliseconds. As this book will demonstrate, stance time is an important element of form because it determines stride rate and thus running velocity. Stance time depends on such form characteristics as foot-strike pattern (forefoot, midfoot, or heel); shank angle (angle of the lower part of the limb—from knee to foot—when the foot makes contact with the ground); relative position of the foot to the body's center of mass upon impact with the ground; and leg stiffness. It is often forgotten that a competitive runner should manipulate form, in an attempt to maximize the ratio of (a) propulsive force created to (b) time on the ground during stance; one is generally looking for higher propulsive forces and shorter contact times as a feature of better form. The time duration of stance and the magnitude of propulsive force are both strongly influenced by form, as will be explained in chapter 8.

Transforming Form

It is clear that certain modes of training can have a positive effect on form. In a profound study, which has become a classic but often-ignored piece of exercise research, Leena Paavolainen and her colleagues at the KIHU Research Institute for Olympic Sports and the University of Jyväskylä (both in Finland) demonstrated that explosive strength training has a major impact on key elements of form and thus distance running performance (18).

In this groundbreaking research, experienced runners altered their training programs by replacing moderate-speed efforts with explosive drills and high-speed running over a nine-week period. The explosive routines included sprints (5–10 × 20–100 meters); jumping exercises (alternative jumps, bilateral counter-movements, drop and hurdle jumps, and one-legged five-jump drills) without additional weight or with a barbell held on the shoulders; and leg-press and knee-extensor-flexor exercises with very low loads and high or maximal movement velocities. Key drills from this research will be featured in chapter 8.

After nine weeks, these runners had reduced their contact times with the ground per step by about 7 percent, without any decrease in step length. This key change in form increased another form element, cadence, by approximately 3.5 percent. Taking more steps per minute while running a 5K, without any decrease in step length, meant that the runners were simply running faster during their 5K races. In fact, they improved 5K race times by an average of 30 seconds. This large improvement was accomplished without any gain in maximal aerobic capacity ($\dot{V}O_2$max) or lactate threshold speed but was associated with enhanced economy. To summarize, the research revealed that appropriate training altered form in a significant way, which in turn led to enhancements in economy and faster 5K times.

This study also showed that the experienced runners had not optimized their form (prior to the research), despite years of training. With the guidance of Paavolainen and colleagues, their form changed significantly in nine weeks; the transformation was associated with enhanced economy and faster 5K running, without an increased risk of injury. It is clear that there is a right way to run, that each runner has in fact not achieved form perfection, and that running technique can be upgraded with appropriate training. This book will provide a comprehensive guide to form-advancing training techniques.

Summary

Traditional views of form have focused on the way the body looks during running, rather than on how changes in the movement patterns of the force-producing parts of the body influence economy, performance, and risk of injury. Another long-term and pervasive belief is that each runner optimizes his own form naturally and therefore does not need to learn how to improve form. These notions have stymied an understanding of optimal running form. Fortunately, a significant body of scientific information is now available to guide runners in their form transformations. It is clear that form alterations—which have positive effects on force production, running economy, performance, and the risk of injury—are desirable. These form transformations will be outlined in this book.

References

1. M.J. Milliron and P.R. Cavanagh, "Sagittal Plane Kinematics of the Lower Extremity During Distance Running," In *Biomechanics of Distance Running*, ed. P.R. Cavanagh (Champaign, IL: Human Kinetics, 1990), 65–106.

2. I.S. Davis, B.J. Bowser, and D.R. Mullineaux, "Greater Vertical Impact Loading in Female Runners With Medically Diagnosed Injuries: A Prospective Investigation," *British Journal of Sports Medicine*, 2015 (downloaded from http://bjsm.com on April 1, 2016).

3. P.R. Cavanagh and K.R. Williams, "The Effect of Stride Length Variation on Oxygen Uptake During Distance Running," *Medicine & Science in Sports & Exercise* 14, no. 1 (1982): 30–35.

4. L.D. Heinert et al., "Effect of Stride Length Variation on Oxygen Uptake During Level and Positive Grade Treadmill Running," *Medicine & Science in Sports & Exercise* 18, no. 2 (1986), 225–230.

5. O. Anderson, *Running Science* (Champaign, IL: Human Kinetics, 2013), 323.

6. P. Larson et al., "Foot Strike Patterns of Recreational and Sub-Elite Runners in a Long-Distance Road Race," *Journal of Sports Science* 29 (2011): 1665–1673.

7. H. Hasegawa, T. Yamauchi, and W.J. Kraemer, "Foot Strike Patterns of Runners at 15-km Point During an Elite-Level Half Marathon," *Journal of Strength and Conditioning Research* 21 (2007): 888–893.

8. D.E. Martin and P.N. Coe, *Training Distance Runners* (Champaign, IL: Leisure Press, 1991), 15–18.

9. Walter Reynolds, interview, April 7, 2016.

10. W.J. Bowerman and W.H. Freeman, *High-Performance Training for Track and Field* (Champaign, IL: Leisure Press, 1991), 88–90.

11. J. Allen, "Proper Running Form," www.runnersworld.com/the-starting-line/proper-running-form (accessed September 28, 2014).

12. J. Daniels, *Daniels' Running Formula* (Third Edition) (Champaign, IL: Human Kinetics, 2014), 27–28.

13. Ibid, p. 28.

14. Ibid.

15. K.P. Clark et al., "Are Running Speeds Maximized With Simple-Spring Stance Mechanics," Journal of Applied Physiology 117, no. 5 (1985), 604-615.

16. S.P. Messier and K.J. Cirillo, "Effects of a Verbal and Visual Feedback System on Running Technique, Perceived Exertion, and Running Economy in Female Novice Runners," *Medicine and Science in Sports and Exercise* 21, no. 2 (1989): S80.

17. K.R. Williams, "Biomechanics of Distance Running," *Current Issues in Biomechanics*, ed. M.D. Grabiner (Champaign, IL: Human Kinetics), 3–31.

18. L. Paavolainen et al., "Explosive Strength Training Improves 5-Km Running Time by Improving Running Economy and Muscle Power," *Journal of Applied Physiology* 86, no. 5 (1999): 1527–1533.

2

Comparing Ordinary and Elite Runners

The average distance runner runs with the same form that Fred Flintstone employed to slam on the brakes in his Stone Age car. Fred did not sweep the ground as he moved his feet; he simply stuck his straight legs out and put his heels on the ground. True, most distance runners don't yell "yabba-dabba-doo!" with each foot-strike, but they do mimic many of the anatomical and neuromuscular elements of Fred's car-stopping pattern as they attempt to move along the ground. Specifically, they land with a relatively straight leg, with the knee approaching a 180-degree angle (a straight line from the waist to the ankle). They also hit the ground heel first, with little backward sweep and the foot well in front of the body (figure 2.1). Fred Flintstone undoubtedly used these straight-leg, heel-striking, ground-impact techniques because he knew they were associated with

Figure 2.1 **Most runners land on their heels, with a nearly straight leg.**

maximal braking forces and thus represented the best way to stop a car suddenly. The average runner uses Flintstone form because he knows no better and because his pattern of running has been corrupted by the modern running shoe.

Ordinary Running Form

If you doubt that heel-striking is so commonplace, consider a study of 514 recreational runners in Sao Paulo, Brazil, in which foot-strike patterns during running were evaluated with a high-speed camera (1). The researchers found that 95 percent of the runners were heel-strikers, landing on their heels as they ran instead of landing on their mid-feet or forefeet (see figure 2.2). Only 21 of the 514 runners (4 percent) were midfoot-strikers, and just four participants (fewer than 1 percent) landed with a forefoot pattern.

In another study, conducted with 936 marathon and half-marathon runners in Manchester, New Hampshire, researchers found that 88.9 percent

Figure 2.2 (*a*) Heel-striking, (*b*) midfoot-striking, and (*c*) forefoot-striking.

of the competitors were heel-strikers, 3.4 percent were midfoot contactors, 1.8 percent were forefoot-strikers, and 5.9 percent featured "discrete foot strike asymmetry"—in other words, the right foot and left foot made contact with the ground differently (2). Although such foot-strike asymmetry might seem odd, it is actually relatively commonplace. Many runners' right and left legs also differ dramatically in other key aspects of form, including the angles with which the legs initially contact the ground and the amounts of swing and sweep that occur between ground contacts (swing and sweep will be explained in more detail later in this chapter).

An intriguing finding in the New Hampshire research was that form and fatigue were linked. Among 286 marathon runners who were observed at both the 10K and 32K points of the marathon, the frequency of heel-striking had increased at the 32K mark, compared with the 10K checkpoint. This is undoubtedly because of the advanced tiredness and augmented muscle, tendon, and skeletal discomfort associated with later stages of the marathon. It also reflects the loss of springiness and energy return properties of marathoners' legs as the race progresses. These marathoners were most likely attempting to rely on their shoes for greater cushioning, energy return, and discomfort protection as their own muscles and tendons became fatigued and thus less protective. As a result, the runners naturally gravitated toward landing on their heels, where midsole cushioning achieves its greatest depth and height (not to mention brightest color).

Such a change in form is understandable. When your legs are tired or feeling weak, it is only natural to want to land on a soft object rather than something a bit harder and less pillowy. However, the truth is that impact forces are actually not reduced by heel-striking, compared with midfoot landing. In fact, peak loading rate (the rate at which impact force increases after first contact with the ground) is actually greater with heel-striking, compared with midfoot landing—even when heel-strikers are wearing "battleship" running shoes with massive heels and midfoot-strikers are running barefoot with no protective cushioning at all. Of course, as shocking at it might seem, unshod runners are cushioned by their natural mechanisms, including the actions of the muscles, tendons, ligaments, and joints after contact with the ground (figure 2.3). Runners sometimes forget that their lower limbs do not have to be treated as weak, high-risk appendages that must be protected by external devices such as running

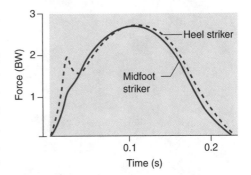

Figure 2.3 **Heel-strike landing with high initial loading rate of impact force and midfoot landing with reduced initial loading rate of impact force.**

shoes. If they are operating correctly, their own legs can be great shock-attenuating structures.

In a separate study of 1,991 participants at the Milwaukee Lakefront Marathon, researchers found that 1,865 (93.7 percent) of the runners, utilized a heel-strike landing pattern (3). Interestingly, in this research the foot-strike pattern was linked to performance: The faster runners in this marathon were much less likely to strike the ground with their heels first, instead tending to be midfoot-strikers. Male and female runners did not experience gender-related differences in foot-strike classification: Both men and women preferred heel-strike conduct on the roads (figure 2.4).

In an outstanding study of 415 runners at a half-marathon in Japan, researchers once again discovered a preference for heel-striking and also found a strong connection between foot-strike pattern and finishing time (4). In this study, heel-striking was detected in "only" 74.9 percent of the athletes, while midfoot-striking was found in a more-salubrious 23.7 percent of participants. However, the relatively low frequency of heel-striking was a result of the inclusion of elite-level runners (including Olympians) in the research. Among the top 69 runners in this race, 36 percent were midfoot-strikers—about seven times the ratio one would expect in a competition with no elite performers.

Figure 2.4 **Both men and women tend to heel-strike.**

In this Japanese study, average contact time with the ground was significantly higher for heel-strikers, compared with midfoot contactors. Heel-strikers spent an average 200 milliseconds on the ground per step, versus just 183 milliseconds for mid- and forefoot-strikers.

It is clear from these latter two studies that foot-strike pattern is an element of form that is strongly related to running speed: Midfoot-strikers tend to be faster than heel-strikers. One reason for this is that superior runners may be more apt to recognize that a heel-striking pattern—with its usually stronger braking forces and longer ground-contact times—has a slowing effect on their running. Another factor is that contact time is in itself strongly related to running speed, since shorter contact times lead directly to higher stride rates. For a runner, maximal speed is the optimal combination of stride rate and stride length as expressed by the equation Running Speed = Stride Rate × Stride Length. The higher the stride rate, the loftier the maximal speed (as long as the increase in stride rate does not shorten stride length). Thus, midfoot-striking, shorter ground-contact times, and faster running are strongly linked.

From a performance standpoint, one can readily see that the two elements of common form discussed so far—landing with straight legs, with the feet well in front of the body, and striking the ground with the heels—are non-optimal. The straight-leg landing directs overall force at landing upward and backward, instead of forward. A runner with such form is commencing the critical, force-producing phase of gait (ground contact) by powerfully pushing himself upward and backward, instead of forward (figure 2.5).

Heel-striking also hurts performance by elongating the stance (contact) phase of running. The ground-contact difference of 17 milliseconds per step (for heel-strikers versus forefoot-strikers)—as detected in the Japanese study—would have a profound effect on performance. Bear in mind that, from the perspective of the foot, a runner moves forward only during the flight phase of gait: During stance, a runner is anchored to the ground and cannot move forward. In fact, a key progression as a runner becomes faster is the partitioning of gait so that less time is spent on the ground and relatively more time is spent flying forward.

Figure 2.5 **The force of heel-striking pushes a runner up and backward instead of forward.**

This becomes a much harder progression for heel-strikers, since they are inherently glued to the ground for a longer time per step, compared with midfoot-strikers.

And the numbers can really add up. Take the case of a heel-striker who runs the 5K in 18:36 (a pace of six minutes per mile, or six minutes per 1.6 kilometers) with a cadence of 170 steps per minute. With each step, he is spending about 17 milliseconds longer than necessary on the ground (compared with midfoot-striking). At first glance, that sounds like very little time lost. However, completing the math reveals that 18.6 minutes × 170 steps per minute × .017 seconds = 53.8 seconds "lost" to glued-on-the-ground foot contact over the duration of the 5K. This runner could be running the 5K in 17:42.2 if he opted for a midfoot landing pattern, all other factors being equal. Another way to examine the situation is to say that the runner is losing 6 × 170 × .017 = 17.3 seconds per mile because of his foot-strike habits.

What Would Kenyans Do?

Not all elite Kenyan runners have perfect form, but the contrast between elite Kenyan runners and running form among non-elite runners could not be more dramatic. Elite Kenyans tend to land with flexed knees rather than straight legs and with the landing foot closer to a position under the body's center of mass, instead of far ahead of the hips and torso (they exhibit large amounts of sweep with each step in order to bring the foot closer to the body at contact). Furthermore, elite Kenyan distance runners tend to land on the midfoot area, instead of sharply on the heel (figure 2.6).

In an informal study carried out at the Kenyan national cross-country championships in Nairobi in 2016, more than 80 percent of the competitors ran with a midfoot landing pattern (compared with the 4 to 5 percent usually observed among non-elite, non-Kenyan runners and the 36 percent observed in the Japanese research completed with elite non-Kenyans) (5).

In contrast with elite Kenyans, elite American runners are much more likely to be heel-strikers. Such notable American runners as Ryan Hall, Kara Goucher, Shalane Flanagan (figure 2.7), and Desiree Linden are (or have been) profound heel-strikers. Not surprisingly, elite American harriers appear to have a higher injury rate, compared with their Kenyan peers. Remember that peak loading rates for impact forces are much higher with heel-striking, compared with midfoot landing, and peak loading rate is a key predictor of running injury. The differences in performance capability do not need to be mentioned here, but remember that heel-striking leads to longer ground-contact times and thus lower stride rates and sub-optimal speeds.

Compared with the average runner, elite Kenyans also have greater sweep of each foot when they run. In other words, the forward-moving swing

Getty Images/Tom Dulat

Figure 2.6   Top-level African runners are nearly always mid-foot strikers.

Getty Images for Rock 'n' Roll Marathon Series/Kent Horner

AFP/Getty Images

Figure 2.7   American distance stars such as Shalane Flanagan (*a*) have been heel-strikers during their careers, whereas top Kenyan athletes such as Olympic gold medalist Eliud Kipoge (*b*) are universally mid-foot strikers.

foot—once it has reached its most advanced forward position—tends to sweep backward toward the ground more dramatically, compared with most runners and even compared with American elites (6) (figure 2.8*a* and *b*).

For now, sweep can be visualized in this way: As a runner moves along, his airborne swing leg and foot move forward ahead of his body. Eventually, the foot stops moving forward relative to the body and is poised to begin moving backward and downward to make contact with the ground. This most-forward position of the foot is referred to as the "still point" (7).

Figure 2.8 In an 8k race, elite Kenyan athlete Caren Maiyo exhibited a maximum shank angle (MSA) of 15 degrees (*a*), and a shank angle at touchdown (SAT) of 3 degrees (*b*), for a lofty sweep of 12 degrees and a "golden ratio" (Sweep/MSA) of 12/15, or .80, which is very typical of top Kenyan runners. In contrast, most elite U.S. distance runners have "rusty ratios" of less than .50. (For information on MSA and SAT see p. 33)

From the still point, a runner's foot has only one place to go: toward the ground. In essence, the foot should be sweeping backward and downward from the still point to make contact with *terra firma*. Fortunately from the standpoint of improving form, this sweeping action can be quantified. It is simply the difference between the maximum angle made by the shin or shank of the leg as it moves forward during swing and the angle made by the shin as the foot makes first contact with the ground (refer back to figure 2.8*a* and *b*). The difference between these two angles is called "sweep."

The average jogger may have a lofty maximal shank angle (the largest angle the shank makes during forward swing of the leg) of 18–22 degrees or so, prior to sweep (figure 2.9), while the elite Kenyan marathoner is commonly at 14 degrees or so (8). (Bear in mind there can be considerable

Figure 2.9 (*a*) Average runner overstriding. (*b*) The average runner, even at slow speed, often reaches an MSA of up to 22 degrees (112 - 90 = 22).

variation among Kenyan elites.) That sounds good for the typical runner, doesn't it? Can't the jogger take longer strides and cover more ground than the elite Kenyan that way? Wouldn't the elite Kenyan be even faster if he would only stretch out his steps a little more?

Unfortunately, when the average runner's foot hits the ground, the shank angle at initial ground contact is likely to be 15 to 16 degrees (9). That is a sweep of a paltry two to three degrees (remember that sweep typically begins at a maximal shank angle of 18 degrees). With a sweep of just two to three degrees, the foot is accelerated toward the ground only minimally. Bear in mind that the force placed on the ground, and thus the propulsive actions that result, depend on the velocity with which the foot hits the ground. Not much velocity can be generated during a two-degree sweep to the ground; it is simply too short to get the leg moving at high speed.

By contrast, elite Kenyans sweep about eight degrees: Although there is considerable variation among elites, the elite Kenyan often starts with a maximum shank angle of 14 degrees and hits the ground with the shank at six degrees or less (10). He can generate a much higher foot velocity during this longer sweep and, therefore, can create a stronger reaction with the ground and an increased amount of propulsive force (figure 2.10a and b).

Don't forget, also, that the braking action created when the foot hits the ground is dependent on shank angle: The greater the angle, the higher the braking force. Excessive Flintstone braking is not ideal when trying to

Figure 2.10 **Kenyan runners do a better job of explosively sweeping the foot back to the ground after it has swung forward, instead of simply letting it fall to the earth.**

run faster and improve performance. So, the form taken up by the average runner (large max shank angle, tiny sweep, foot contact well ahead of the body) is conducive to braking and slow speed, while the form adopted by the elite Kenyan (more expansive sweep, foot contact closer to the body) is appropriate for creating greater propulsive forces against the ground and faster running.

Kenyan Cadence

Compared to average runners, elite Kenyans also run with a higher cadence, or the number of steps taken per minute. Research and anecdotal observation have revealed that the average runner has a stepping rate of about 160 steps per minute at a variety of speeds (11). In contrast, elite Kenyans (and elite runners in general) run with a cadence of about 180 to 200 steps per minute (12).

The implications of this difference are obvious. As mentioned previously, running speed is simply the product of stride rate and stride length, as expressed by the equation Velocity = Stride Rate × Stride Length. Maximal velocity is directly linked with distance-running performance and is obtained through an optimal combination of stride rate and stride length. Anything that thwarts the development of a higher stride rate—for example, heel-striking and landing with the foot far ahead of the body—will hamper the improvement of maximal speed and therefore performance.

Importantly, shank angle at initial contact with the ground (SAT) also tends to be significantly different between the elite Kenyan and average runner. Bear in mind that shank angle at contact with the ground can vary tremendously among all runners. A large shank angle of 16 to 18 degrees or more at touchdown will lead to strong, drawn-out braking forces when the foot is on the ground. This can be attributed to the initial production of upward- and backward-directed vector forces and also the time required to move the foot relative to the body to produce forward-horizontal propulsive force. (It is impossible to produce forward propulsive force when the foot is ahead of the body.) A smaller shank angle of about six degrees at contact will decrease braking forces and reduce the time required to end the braking phase of stance and move into forward-horizontal force-production mode. A negative shank angle at ground contact means that essentially no braking force is produced but also signifies that the runner is on the brink of falling on his face.

While shank angles at initial ground contact of approximately 16 degrees are frequently observed in average runners, shank angles at first ground contact range from zero to seven degrees in most elite Kenyans. Fortunately, initial shank angle is highly trainable and can be made more Kenyan-like in runners of all ability and experience levels, from the novice jogger to even the most road-toughened and experienced high-shank-angled American runner.

The amazingly high frequency of heel-striking among non-Kenyan runners has suggested to some running observers that the heel-strike, ground-contact mode is the normal and healthy way to run. In this view, it appears elite Kenyan runners have developed a specialized way of interacting with the ground, a way that is unnatural but necessary for their trade as professional athletes (just as professional baseball pitchers hold and throw the ball differently compared with the novice baseball player in the street).

However, careful investigation reveals such thinking is in error. In the 1950s, research conducted with high-speed video cameras revealed that almost all runners in the study contacted the ground with the midfoot or forefoot, with the mode of contact dependent on preferred competitive distance. As race distance increased (and therefore race speed declined), runners tended to land on the midfoot; as competitive distance shortened and race velocity increased they tended to land on the forefoot (13).

What has caused the human race to evolve so rapidly in this way in only 50 years or so, with nearly complete abandonment of forefoot- and midfoot-striking and the rise of a new class of humans who prefer banging the ground with their heels?

It is likely that the advent of the modern running shoe has produced this corruption of form. Although there has been a recent trend toward the use of minimal running shoes and even a movement advocating the adoption of an unshod running style, the *au courant* running shoe—the kind of running shoe to which most customers are directed by watchful store merchants—remains a kind of heavy, highly colorful, and creatively designed "battle wagon" in which a runner's feet are to be embedded. In particular, the modern running shoe has a raised heel with an especially thick layer of bright-hued foam underneath.

Researchers at Harvard University have recently pointed out that runners who usually run barefoot are almost never heel-strikers; in fact, they usually make first contact with the ground with the forefoot or midfoot (14). In contrast, runners who are accustomed to running in modern shoes almost always hit the ground heel-first (15).

I have taken extensive videos of Kenyan children playing and running and have reached similar conclusions (16). The frequency of heel-striking among barefoot Kenyan children during running is nearly zero, whereas the frequency of heel-striking rises significantly for Kenyan children wearing up-to-date footwear—especially for those wearing modern running shoes with colossal heels. One can only conclude that running shoes with large heels "push" runners toward landing on the cushioned spots of the shoes, places where the most foam is piled into the midsole and where the landing feels softest and safest (even though it actually is not).

How have elite Kenyan runners managed to evade this undesirable heel-striking pattern? After all, they also wear modern running shoes with big heels, especially during training, and many up-and-coming Kenyan athletes yearn for a shoe-company contract and the opportunity to be provided with free big-heelers year-round.

An often-forgotten factor is that most elite Kenyan runners start their running careers very early in life, running intensely over the Kenyan countryside—unshod (figure 2.11). It is likely that such runners develop not only tremendous foot and ankle strength as a result of their barefoot running, but also become locked into a running style that features midfoot ground contacts. After all, few young runners would want the force of impact against roots, sharp stones, fragments of glass, and hard dirt to fall solely on their heels; it is simply too painful. Rather, young, Kenyan, soon-to-be-elite harriers learn to distribute impact forces around the foot by landing with a midfoot-contact pattern. They probably also develop superior "proprioception" by running in this way, or an enhanced ability to feel the way in which the foot is interacting with the ground and to react accordingly during force production. It is unlikely that these advantages would be abandoned completely in favor of landing on colorful mush with just the heel.

Figure 2.11   Young Kenyan runners often train barefoot.

Kenyan Running Posture

Postural elements are also different between elite Kenyan runners and all average runners. During running, posture entails the relative positions of the head, neck, and trunk (straight, curved forward, or curved backward) and also the positioning and actions of the arms and the rotation of the trunk during forward movement (17). In general, the elite Kenyan has a straighter posture (with head, neck, and trunk in a straight line rather than hunched forward or stretched backward), compared with the average harrier. Kenyan arm movement tends to be more economical, with less "winginess" and much less vertical lifting of the arms. Rather, the arms tend to swing naturally like pendulums with little muscular effort. Finally, the best Kenyans tend to avoid wash-tub-like, energy-wasting, speed-demoting rotations of the trunk, even at high speeds. Techniques for developing optimal posture will be discussed fully in chapter 10.

The reasons for (and outcomes of) these differences in foot-strike pattern, sweep, cadence, shank angle at ground contact, and posture will be discussed fully in this book. Note that the average runner is not expected to move biomechanically with the exact patterns of (or the same running speeds as) an elite Kenyan runner. But these disparities in form have profound implications for running economy, risk of injury, and running performance and thus help create guidelines for establishing better form for both the average and elite runner.

Summary

The form of the average runner differs in a number of key ways from the form adopted by the fastest runners in the world. The average runner demonstrates very little sweeping action with each foot and tends to hit the ground on her heel, with a relatively straight leg, and with the foot well ahead of her center of mass. This pattern is reinforced by the modern running shoe, with its high, big-heeled construction pushing runners toward heel-strikes.

In contrast, Kenyan elite runners are the world's best sweepers and favor midfoot-strikes with less-straight legs and with the foot closer to the center of mass. This gait pattern is linked with the greatest performance possibilities and the least likelihood of injury.

References

1. M O de Almeida et al., "Is the Rearfoot Pattern the Most Frequently Used Foot Strike Pattern Among Recreational Shod Distance Runners?" *Physical Therapy in Sport* 16, no. 1 (2015): 29–33.

2. P. Larson et al., "Foot Strike Patterns of Recreational and Sub-Elite Runners in a Long-Distance Road Race," *Journal of Sports Sciences* 29, no. 15 (2011): 1665–1673.

3. M.E. Kasmer et al., "Foot-Strike Pattern and Performance in a Marathon," *International Journal of Sports Physiology and Performance* 8, no. 3 (2013): 286–292.

4. H. Hasegawa, T. Yamauchi, and W.J. Kraemer, "Foot Strike Patterns of Runners at the 15-km Point During an Elite-Level Half Marathon," *Journal of Strength and Conditioning Research* 21, no. 3 (2007): 888–893.

5. Owen Anderson, unpublished video analysis of the event (2016).

6. Walter Reynolds, personal communication based on video analysis of hundreds of elite and ordinary runners, July 7, 2017.

7. Walter Reynolds, personal communication, July 7, 2017.

8. Ibid.

9. Ibid.

10. Ibid.

11. J.F. Hafer et al. "The Effect of a Cadence Retraining Protocol on Running Biomechanics and Efficiency: A Pilot Study," *Journal of Sports Sciences* 33, no. 7 (2014): 1–8.

12. J. Daniels, *Daniels' Running Formula* (Third Edition) (Champaign, IL: Human Kinetics, 2014), 26.

13. T. Nett, "Foot Plant in Running," *Track Technique* 15 (1964): 462–463.

14. D.E. Lieberman et al., "Foot Strike Patterns and Collision Forces in Habitually Barefoot Versus Shod Runners," *Nature* 462 (2010): 531–535.

15. Ibid.

16. Owen Anderson, unpublished video taken in Kenya (2011–2012).

17. Walter Reynolds, personal communication, August 1, 2017.

3

Elements of Form

When two objects collide, the result is pure physics. This is true whether the two objects are vehicles speeding down a freeway, billiard balls rolling along a felt table top, or a runner colliding with the ground with each step, 180 times per minute.

The specific characteristics of those encounters between the ground and a runner's foot determine how fast an athlete can run, yet most runners devote very little time to working on their "collision dynamics." While runners concern themselves with such variables as weekly mileage, long-run distance, running speed, heart rate, and the composition of interval workouts, they often ignore the fact that running capacity depends on the quality of a runner's interactions with the ground and that the outcome of any collision depends on the angles with which objects strike each other. People know this is true when they play billiards but disregard the principle when they run. They are usually not concerned at all about the angles their legs and feet make with respect to the ground at impact—even though some angles are strongly linked to the highest production of propulsive force and the lowest risk of injury, while other angles produce excessive braking forces and increase the chances of getting hurt.

By running the way they've always run and believing their naturally adopted gait is best, most runners don't stress over the exact point of impact with the ground (whether they are hitting the ground with the heel, midfoot, or forefoot), even though choosing the wrong impact area is linked with both higher braking forces and the transfer of injury, producing force at greater rates through the legs. And few runners consider the stiffness of their legs at impact, yet stiffness has a significant effect on collision force patterns. For example, the firmer the ground, the greater the force that is transferred back to the runner's leg after impact. The stiffer the leg, the greater the force that is pushed into the ground to provide propulsion.

With respect to collision angles of the leg and foot, points of impact with the ground, and leg stiffness, an individual runner's collisions with the ground are predictable and repeatable. And since no runner (not even Usain Bolt) can move with the speed of light, Newton's Laws of Motion apply to the outcomes of the collisions, regardless of the athlete's training volume, heart rate, or aerobic capacity. Newton's Third Law is especially important from the standpoint of collision forces and running speed: It tells us that if a runner's foot hits the ground while the leg is relatively straight and the foot is in front of the body, that foot will push down and forward on the ground, and the ground will push *up and back* on the athlete's leg and body.

As Newton said, "For every action, there is an equal and opposite reaction." And the opposite reaction in this case is exactly what the runner does not want, since the forces are directed in opposition to his desired path of movement. In other words, the runner wants to move forward, but his collision with the ground is directing him upward and backward (figure 3.1).

Figure 3.1 When a runner strikes the ground with her heel, well in front of her body, the initial impact (and thus propulsive) forces are directed upward and backward, away from the direction of movement desired by the runner.

When a runner hits the ground with the wrong leg angle, Newton's laws suggest that the resulting forces must be non-optimal and that the runner can never achieve his best possible running speeds. Therefore, it is imperative for the runner to learn to use the correct collision angle; this is an essential element of good form.

The critical angle of impact is called "shank angle" and is determined by the angle the shank makes with the ground at initial impact. Shank angle is measured at the exact moment the foot makes first contact with the running surface. To determine shank angle, a line is drawn from the center of the knee, parallel with the shank, directly to the ground. Another line is then drawn straight forward along the ground, from the point at which the line parallel with the shank touches the ground. Then, 90 degrees are subtracted from this angle to reveal the actual shank angle, which is therefore the angle between the shank and a line perpendicular with the ground at the point of impact.

For example, let's say that the angle between the ground and shank at first impact is 100 degrees (figure 3.2). The actual shank angle is $100 - 90 = 10$ degrees. (Remember that the shank angle is actually the angle between a line drawn perpendicular with the ground at the point of impact and the shank itself.)

A shank angle can be positive, neutral, or negative. If the shin is inclined forward from the knee when the foot makes contact with the ground, the shank angle is positive (figure 3.3). If the shank is perfectly perpendicular with the ground when the foot hits the ground, the shank angle is neutral, or zero degrees (figure 3.4).

Figure 3.2 **Shank angle is the angle between the shank and a line drawn perpendicular to the ground at the point of impact.**

If the shank is inclined backward from the knee at the time of impact, the shank angle is negative by definition. In this situation, the total angle between

Figure 3.3 **When the shank is inclined forward from the knee at the moment of impact, the shank angle is positive.**

the ground and the shank is going to be less than 90 degrees. If we say it is 84 degrees, then the shank angle at first impact will be 84 – 90 = negative 6 degrees (figure 3.5), and the athlete is in effect falling forward at impact with the ground.

Figure 3.4 When the shank is perpendicular to the ground at the moment of impact, the shank angle is neither positive or negative—it is zero.

Figure 3.5 When the shank is inclined backward from the knee at the moment of impact, the shank angle is negative.

The Paradox of Small, Positive Shank Angles

Why is shank angle at initial impact (also called shank angle at touchdown, or SAT) an absolutely critical element of running form, even though it has never been mentioned as such—anywhere—prior to publication of this book? As Sir Isaac Newton pointed out more than 300 years ago, the angle at which two objects collide with each other determines the directions of the forces created. A negative shank angle, with the leg pushing down and back on the ground and thus the ground pushing ahead and up on the leg and body, would appear to be optimal during running (but read chapter 11 to find out why this is actually not the case). In theory, a neutral, zero-degree shank angle might be very good because it would allow a runner to bounce forward elastically and economically (like a basketball bouncing along a court), with very little braking force during each impact with the ground. Positive shank angles would appear to be sub-optimal since they bring significant braking forces into play, especially at larger shank angles in which braking forces on the body are directed upward and backward fairly dramatically. The bottom line is that shank angle determines the braking and propulsive forces that are present when a runner's foot hits the ground. Thus, shank angle is critically important, since it determines forward velocity. As it turns out, shank angle also has a strong effect on the risk of injury, with large, positive shank angles significantly raising the chance of getting hurt. Somewhat surprisingly, though, small, positive shank angles are actually optimal.

There is no gene for shank angle, and therefore it is not genetically determined. It is controlled by environmental factors and extremely subject to corruption by the modern running shoe. It is certainly not set at its optimal position in all runners. In fact, most runners run with horrible shank angles at impact, which both slows them down and magnifies their probability of injury. Fortunately, shank angle is trainable, and—this is critical—it should be trained, despite the popular, but misguided, view that a runner runs the way he runs and nothing should be done about it. As a key element of running form, shank angle can be adjusted and made optimal with the use of some superb running-form drills that teach the nervous system how to control the angle of the shank with the ground at impact. These drills will be fully described in chapter 7. It seems likely that Isaac Newton would be proud of this use of his Third Law.

The Importance of Maximum Shank Angle

In addition to SAT, there is another angle relevant and critically important to form: maximum shank angle. Unlike SAT, which is measured when the foot makes initial contact with the ground, maximum shank angle is determined during the swing phase of gait, when the foot is airborne and moving ahead of the body. In fact, maximum shank angle is usually measured when the foot has reached its farthest point forward relative to the body during forward swing of the leg. To calculate maximum shank angle, a line is again drawn from the knee to the foot, completely parallel with the shank itself. Another line is drawn parallel with the ground from the bottom end of the shank (knee-to-foot line); the angle between these lines is computed (figure 3.6). Once again, 90 degrees is subtracted from this angle to determine maximum shank angle. In figure 3.6, the maximum shank angle for the runner would be $114 - 90 = 24$ degrees

Figure 3.6 Maximum shank angle is the largest angle the shank makes during forward swing of the leg.

Why is maximum shank angle an important element of running form, even though—like SAT—it has never before been described in a book, article, blog, video, or app? For one thing, maximum shank angle can be related to step length, which is an important performance variable determined by form. Step length is one of the two essential factors that determines running speed, the other being step rate. The equation for this is simply Running Speed = Step Rate (steps per second) × Step Length (in meters). For example, a runner moving along with a step rate of three steps per second and a step length (distance between steps) of 2 meters per step would be running at a speed of 6 meters per second, or a tempo of $400/6 = 66.7$ seconds per 400 meters. Maximal running speed, a strong predictor of distance-running performance (and of course sprint performance too), is the optimal combination of step rate and step length, and step length can be strongly associated with maximum shank angle. As an aside, this association can occur for two different reasons:

1. A less skilled runner might simply allow the foot to plop onto the ground after a large forward swing and with a hefty maximum shank angle, thus creating a rather long (but sub-optimal) step length—sub-optimal because of the backward-directed propulsive forces and the corresponding negative effect on step rate.

2. A more accomplished runner might accelerate the foot dramatically back toward the ground after achieving a big maximum shank angle and thus transfer an impressive amount of kinetic energy into the ground (more than could be attained with a small maximum shank angle). This causes the body to fly forward farther and correspondingly creates a relatively long step length.

Maximum shank angle is very important for another reason: It has a direct impact on another critically important form variable called reversal of swing (ROS), or the difference between maximum shank angle (MSA) and shank angle at touchdown (SAT). For example, if a runner has an MSA of 15 degrees and an SAT of three degrees, by definition his ROS is then $15 - 3 = 12$ degrees (refer back to figure 2.8*a* and *b*). In other words, the runner has swept his foot back 12 degrees from the maximum position prior to collision with the ground; he has reversed maximal swing by 12 degrees.

ROS is another essential element of form. Picture a runner's foot, either the right or left, as it moves through the entire gait cycle, from toe-off through airborne swing, then back to the ground via ROS, and then through the stance phase of gait with a return to toe-off. What would a diagram of the foot's pattern of movement look like?

The Kidney Bean in Your Stride

If you answered "a rectangle," it is a good thing that you purchased this book—as your concept of running form needs some updating. If you answered "an oval," you are getting closer and deserve at least a "C" on your running-form exam. But in fact, as famed German running coach Winfried Vonstein has pointed out, the actual trajectory of the foot is shaped like a kidney bean (1) (figure 3.7).

As shown in figure 3.7, after toe-off the foot moves backward and upward, then starts forward and takes a little downward dip, producing the concavity on the top side of the kidney bean. It then moves upward and forward until it reaches its farthest distance ahead of the body, at which point maximum shank angle (MSA) is measured. From the point of maximum shank angle, the foot then starts back toward the body and downward toward the ground before making impact with *terra firma* at SAT. The movement of the shank and foot from the most-forward point to initial ground contact is the ROS and the subsequent phase of gait is sometimes referred to as the "clawing" (or pawing) action of the foot on the ground. The foot remains on the ground (the "stance" phase of gait) as the body passes overhead before once again toeing

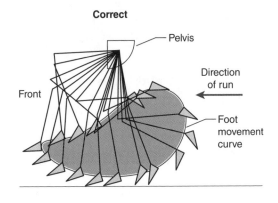

Figure 3.7 **The foot has a kidney bean shaped flight path during running.**

off and moving upward and backward. The overall pathway of the foot traces the shape of a kidney bean in almost every runner.

As Vonstein has pointed out, this has some implications for proper pelvic position during running. For example, if the bottom of the pelvis is tilted backward (and thus the top of the pelvis is tipped forward), the foot's acrobatics change and the kidney bean can spoil and become rotten (figure 3.8, and also see figure 1.1b). Specifically, the ability of the foot to move forward is crippled when the top of the pelvis tips forward, as this decreases MSA, ROS, and almost certainly running velocity. The capacity of the foot to move backward is enhanced when the bottom of the pelvis is back—but this produces no positive gain in running speed (in effect, it reduces the magnitude of vertical propulsive forces, which, as we will see in subsequent chapters, are so critical for speed). In contrast, if the pelvis is aligned vertically, with no significant forward or rearward tilt, maximum shank angle is not harmed, and stride length and ROS are not impaired (figure 3.9).

Figure 3.8 A pelvis which is tilted forward can thwart MSA, ROS, and SAT.

Figure 3.9 An upright pelvis does not harm MSA, ROS, or SAT.

Sir Isaac Newton and Your Next Marathon or 10K

As mentioned, the movement downward and backward of the foot to the ground, starting from the point at which the foot has reached its farthest point ahead of the body, is called sweep or reversal of swing (ROS). The foot hits the ground at the end of ROS, and that is when Newtonian kinetic energy must be considered if a runner wants to move along with optimal form and speed. Though Sir Isaac was not much of a marathoner or cross-country runner, he rightly pointed out that the kinetic energy of an object is the energy the object possesses as a result of its movement. We can apply this to running; in this case, the object that is moving is obviously the runner's leg and foot. The work that the leg and foot carry out as the foot makes contact with the ground determines the forward propulsive forces created and thus the speed of the runner. And that work is a direct function of the kinetic energy of the leg; the greater the kinetic energy, the greater the work done on the ground and the higher the propulsive force that can be developed.

The equation for this phenomenon is simply $E_k = \frac{1}{2} mv^2$, where E_k is the kinetic energy of the leg and foot, $\frac{1}{2}$ is a constant, m is the mass of the leg and foot, and v is the velocity of the leg and foot. From this equation it is possible to see that the kinetic energy of the leg during running, and specifically during ROS, is determined by the leg's velocity. Expressed another way, the work that the foot and leg can do on the ground, and thus the propulsive force that can be created, depends on the ROS velocity of the leg and its attached foot. In fact, work and force depend on the square of the velocity of the leg (as can be seen in the equation), which means when the velocity of the leg during ROS doubles, the kinetic energy of the leg quadruples.

The importance of ROS is readily apparent. Yet the average distance runner has an MSA of about 18 degrees and an SAT of only 16 degrees. Yes, that's right: His ROS is an outrageously small two degrees (figure 3.10).

Very little velocity can be generated from such a small ROS. Further, when the velocity of the leg is generated during only two degrees of movement, the leg has very little kinetic energy as it approaches the ground and very little propulsive force can be created via ground contact. Yet this is the way the vast majority of distance runners move along the ground, with tiny doses of ROS and large SATs. Instead of creating large propulsive force, they are generating mega quantities of braking force. This helps explain why average runners are so slow. It would all seem a little depressing—except that ROS and SAT and thus the forces the leg applies to the ground are responsive to proper form training. Specifically, the drills outlined in this book will dramatically upgrade ROS and SAT and lead to significantly faster running.

What is the ROS of Usain Bolt, the world's fastest human in 2017? It is close to insane, as Bolt usually prefers an ROS of about 21 degrees or so when he runs 100 meters at top speed. (His maximum shank angle is often about 28 degrees when he sprints 100 meters, and his ground-contact shank angle is frequently close to 7 degrees, creating an ROS of 21 degrees, or 75 percent of maximal shank angle (2).) Over the course of those 21 degrees, an amazing amount of velocity is generated, resulting in a high level of kinetic energy that can be transformed into force-generating work against the ground. Elite marathon runners, of course, don't have to generate such "Bolts" of lightning as they run at their relatively slower paces. For example, when Dennis

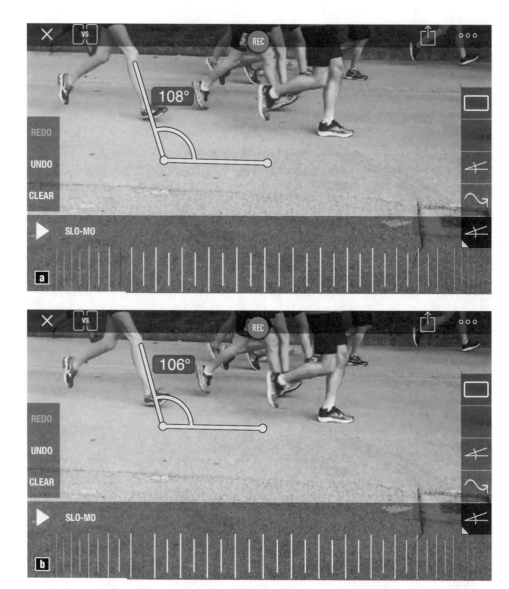

Figure 3.10 (*a*) This very typical runner has an MSA of 18 (108 - 90) and (*b*) an SAT of 16 (106 - 90). Thus, ROS is only two degrees, and a ridiculously small amount of kinetic energy imparted to the ground at impact.

Kimetto set the men's world record for the marathon, he employed an average ROS of about 8 degrees (from 14 at MSA to 6 at SAT) (3)—just over one-third as much as Bolt yet four times as much as the average distance runner.

ROS to Maximum Shank Angle Ratio

This discussion of maximum shank angle and reversal of swing leads us to another critical, quantifiable form variable: the ratio of Reversal of Swing to maximum shank angle, or ROS/MSA. This variable tells us how effectively a runner is using his swing—in other words, once he "loads his gun" (puts his foot out in front of his body), how much of that loading process is used to place propulsive force on the ground. In most cases, the higher the ratio (ROS/MSA), the better the force applied to the ground.

Take the case of the average runner we previously mentioned, who swings out 18 degrees but reverses that swing and moves the high leg back by only two degrees before hitting the ground, producing a minuscule ROS/MSA of 2/18, or .11. Essentially, she is moving her leg and foot back only 11 percent of the distance she moved them forward, and thus is producing only a minor amount of desired propulsive force on the ground. Furthermore, with her foot so far ahead of the body (since she has not come back the remaining 89 percent), she is producing huge braking forces with each ground collision.

How much better she would be as a runner if she would sweep halfway back, hitting the ground with an SAT of 9 degrees, thus producing an ROS/MSA of 9/18 = .5? There would be considerably less braking force, with the foot not so far ahead of the body, and much more propulsive force because of the greater kinetic energy developed by the leg during sweep.

She would be even better yet with a larger ROS, coming back to an SAT of about 6 degrees, thus producing an ROS/MSA of 12/18 = .67. This would decrease braking force, since the foot would be closer to the body at impact and would simultaneously increase propulsive force, thanks to the increase in Newtonian kinetic energy.

You might think that a full sweep back to an SAT of 0 degrees would be optimal, since it would minimize braking force. That is logical; however, this creates a situation in which the shank is not at the proper angle when maximal propulsive force is created.

In fact, research carried out by noted running-form expert Walt Reynolds suggests that the optimal ROS/MSA (from the standpoint of creating the highest running speeds) is approximately .7 to .75 (3). In other words, after you swing out with your foot, you should sweep back and reverse the swing by about 75 percent of the swing distance before making contact with the ground. A ratio lower than .75 expands braking forces and decreases forward propulsive forces; a higher ratio tends to decrease forward propulsive forces as well.

Foot-Strike Pattern

The way the foot itself strikes the ground is yet another essential component of form. In a forefoot-strike the initial contact of the foot with the ground is toward the front portion of the shoe, with no heel contact at initial foot-strike. A midfoot-strike is one in which roughly the middle region of the shoe makes first contact with the ground, with the heel contacting the ground shortly thereafter. A heel-strike, also known as rear-foot strike, is one in which the first contact of the shoe with the ground is made in the heel area (4).

Foot-strike pattern is an important element of form because it affects the duration of the stance phase of gait and thus another important form variable: cadence, or the number of steps taken per minute, which is one version of step rate. Foot-strike pattern also shapes the velocity and magnitude of impact forces that travel up the leg after the foot collides with the ground.

Heel-striking does not fare well from the standpoints of stance duration and the "loading rate" of force (the rate at which force on the leg increases after impact). Heel-striking tends to expand the duration of stance by about one-hundredth of a second, compared with midfoot- or forefoot-striking. While this might seem small, those hundredths of seconds, which are unnecessarily wasted on the ground, add up over time. In the case of a heel-striking runner taking 180 steps per minute while running one mile (or 1.6 kilometers) in five minutes, the equation 5 minutes × 180 steps per minute × .01 seconds = 9 seconds shows he is unnecessarily glued to the ground for a significant amount of time. In other words, he has the potential to reduce his time from 5:00 to 4:51 simply by changing from heel- to midfoot-striking. If he is running the half-marathon, the gains would be even greater: 13.1 miles × 9 seconds per mile = 117.9 seconds "lost" on the ground because of heel-striking, which can potentially be retrieved by shifting to midfoot-striking. An improvement in time of 1:57 could be achieved, which would be a huge gain for a near-elite male competitor, in this case from 65:30 to 63:33.

Of course, the gains for a non-elite runner could be even greater. Take the case of a half-marathon runner moving along at 8 minutes per mile with a cadence of 180 steps per minute and a heel-strike pattern. The equation 8 × 180 × .01 seconds = 14.4 seconds per mile shows he is spending an excessive amount of time on the ground per mile. Per the equation 13.1 × 14.4 = 188.6 seconds, he is 3 minutes and 8 seconds slower than he could be if he were using midfoot-striking.

A beginning runner moving along at a relatively slow speed spends about 70 percent of his time on the ground while running and 30 percent of his time flying forward, whereas the fastest humans spend only 39 percent of their time on the ground with 61 percent of their time in flight. Shifting from heel-striking to midfoot-striking can help the average runner make the transition to more flight time with less stance time and attain higher training speeds, greater overall fitness, and faster competitive running velocities.

Compared to midfoot-striking, heel-striking also has a dramatic effect on the way impact forces are experienced by the foot, leg, hips, and spine. Specifically, heel-striking creates a greater "impact transient," meaning impact force travels up the leg more quickly with a heel-strike pattern, compared with midfoot-striking. In fact, heel-striking creates a quick spike of impact force that hammers the leg, compared with the less traumatic and more even distribution of force associated with midfoot-striking (see figure 2.3 in chapter 2).

The loftier impact transient associated with heel-striking creates a greater risk of injury, compared with midfoot-striking. Fortunately, like SAT, MSA, and ROS, foot-strike pattern is highly trainable. This is especially fortunate, since approximately 95 percent of distance runners are confirmed heel-strikers. Another term, foot angle at touchdown (FAT) describes what the foot is doing at initial impact with the ground. There will be more information about FAT in subsequent chapters (figure 3.11).

Figure 3.11 **FAT is simply the angle the foot makes at initial impact with the ground.**

Cadence and Lean

As mentioned previously, cadence (one version of step rate) is simply the number of steps taken per minute during running. Cadence is fundamentally important for running performance because it is one of the two variables that determines running speed, the other being step length.

During quality workouts and competitions, elite runners always move along with a cadence of at least 180 steps per minute, suggesting that it is a kind of threshold for cadence which should be strived for by runners hoping to improve their training and competitive speeds. A higher cadence generally means that a runner is spending less time on the ground per step and thus has the potential to achieve greater relative flight times and distances and higher running speeds.

Cadence is linked with other form variables. For example, midfoot-strikers tend to have a naturally higher cadence, compared with heel-strikers. In fact, if you require a runner to move along with a higher cadence than usual, he will almost always automatically shift toward a midfoot-strike pattern (if he is normally a heel-striker). Runners who slightly lean forward from the ankles during the stance phase of gait also tend to have a higher cadence (figure 3.12), compared with upright runners and those unfortunate souls who actually lean backward while attempting to run the 5K or marathon.

If the runner is leaning forward, the lean is positive. If she is completely upright and perpendicular to the ground, the lean is neutral. If she is leaning backward, the lean is negative. Slight forward lean is preferred because it is believed that, in conformity with Newton's Laws of Motion, propulsive force applied to the ground travels through the body in the direction of the body, and it is better that the force be applied upward and forward, rather than straight upward, or upward and backward. Excessive forward lean could, of course, reduce step length; it is believed that a forward lean of about 5 percent is close to optimal.

Figure 3.12 Lean is simply the angle made by the body with respect to a line drawn perpendicular to the ground at the heel during stance.

Posture

As Walt Reynolds has pointed out (3), running posture is composed of three key elements: arm action and placement; trunk rotation; and the relative positions of the head, neck, and trunk with respect to each other.

Among a group of one thousand runners, the arms are held and moved in one thousand different ways. However, it is clear that certain arm habits have a negative impact on running performance and that there is a most economical way to use the arms during gait. For example, "winginess," or holding the arms out to the sides, cannot be a positive, since it forces the runner to expend energy keeping the arms laterally suspended. Similarly, large looping actions of the arms tend to be rather slow movements; if a runner learns to run in this way, his legs will usually move slowly in parallel with the upper limbs, producing a meager cadence. Arms with big swing (associated with their active, energy-using, concentric contractions of the shoulder muscles) are also energetically costly, compared to a situation in which the arms simply swing back and forth like nearly friction-free pendulums suspended from the shoulders. It is important for distance runners to note that their $\dot{V}O_2$max (maximal aerobic capacity) is not an infinite variable. It makes little sense to eat up a significant fraction of that $\dot{V}O_2$max during running as a result of arm action. The available oxygen should be used by the part of the body that actually produces forward propulsion—notably the core, legs, and feet.

It is clear that the most economical pattern of movement of the arms can be recommended without trepidation, especially since the modern runner realizes that the arms do not provide propulsive force. An economical pattern involves a simple, straight-ahead swinging action of the arms from the shoulders, with the hands beside the hips at the end of the arm backswing and the elbows beside the hips at the end of the forward swing of the arms. Furthermore, since long levers are more costly to move back and forth than short levers, and since the arms are indeed levers, it would appear optimal to shorten the levers by initiating 90-degree angles at the elbows and then moving the hands roughly halfway to the shoulders during running (figure 3.13 and 3.14).

The economy principle also applies to rotational actions of the trunk during running. It makes little sense to rotate the trunk significantly, like a washing machine, clockwise and counter-clockwise, as a runner moves along. The greater the rotation, the larger the energy expenditure. "Washtubbing" is also evidence that a runner has a weak core. While it is natural for the right arm to move ahead as the left knee drives forward during gait, it is not natural or economical for the trunk to rotate counter-clockwise significantly to accomplish a counter-balance to the forward movement of the left leg. In other words, forward leg movement should not perturb body balance so much that a dramatic counter-rotation of the trunk is required to

Figure 3.13 **The 90-degree position of the elbows.**

Figure 3.14 **The halfway position, with the hands moved toward the shoulders.**

achieve balance. A relatively still trunk is preferred. This is attained through diligent training of the core and by paying attention to what the trunk is doing during running.

Finally, upper body posture can be determined by taking video of a runner and then placing points (on a still image from the video) at the center of the runner's head, the center of her neck, and the centers of her thorax and hips. When the dots are connected, the line should be straight. If it is not straight, the runner is moving along with her upper body hunched forward or leaning backward, neither of which is optimal (figure 3.15). Hunching the upper body forward tends to decrease step length and thwart the attainment of the types of speeds that can be obtained with a straighter posture. Leaning the upper body backward tends to push the feet out in front of the center of mass, which increases braking forces whenever a foot hits the ground.

Figure 3.15 **Hunching the body forward tends to decrease step length and reduce running speed.**

Fortunately, all three postural elements—arm action; trunk rotation; and head, neck, and trunk position—can be optimized by the drills described later in this book.

Summary

For the first time in running history, running form can be quantified and then developed and coached in a proper way. The key variables of form are maximum shank angle (MSA), shank angle at touchdown (SAT), foot angle at touchdown (FAT), reversal of swing (ROS), and the ratio of ROS to MSA (ROS/MSA). These essential variables can be measured easily by runners and coaches and then improved steadily over time to produce optimal running form. Such form will produce a "collision physics" of running that simultaneously optimizes propulsive forces, minimizes braking forces, and controls the rate at which impact forces are transferred through the leg and body (thereby decreasing the risk of injury).

References

1. W. Vonstein, "Some Reflections on Maximum Speed Sprinting Technique," *New Studies in Athletics* 11, no. 2–3 (1996): 161–165.

2. Owen Anderson, personal observation, July 7, 2017

3. Walt Reynolds, video analysis, July 7, 2017

4. P. Larson et al., "Foot Strike Patterns of Recreational and Sub-Elite Runners in a Long-Distance Road Race," *Journal of Sports Sciences*, 29, no. 15 (2011): 1665–1673.

4

How Form Can Enhance Performance and Prevent Injury

The goals of form improvement include reducing the risk of injury, upgrading performance, and fine-tuning running economy. Another positive, though not automatic, benefit of form improvement is that it often creates a smoother-looking running style. Instead of bumps and jerks due to heel-striking ahead of the body, optimal form involves bouncing rhythmically from foot to foot, giving the appearance of efficiency and grace. It can also feel much more powerful because of the reduction in horizontal braking force during each contact with the ground. The larger fraction of stance devoted to horizontal propulsive force, the more effective use of elastic energy to provide forward propulsion, and the better timing of vertical propulsive force (it will reach a peak at a more optimal time, when the foot is not still in front of the body) are all aspects of good form.

Running Form and Injury Prevention

More than 19 million people finish road races in the United States annually, and around 54 million Americans engage in running at some point over the course of a year (1). Amazingly, 30 million individuals run or jog at least 50 days yearly in the United States, and there are about 540,000 marathon finishers and nearly two million half-marathon finishers annually (2). These encouraging facts are tempered by the realities that approximately 65 percent of regular runners are injured (3) and up to 92 percent of marathon trainees end up on the shelf (4) for some significant period of time during the year.

Science suggests that the use of proper running form can lower these injury rates significantly. From an injury standpoint, the key problems with common form—the kind of heel-strike, foot-ahead-of-the-body form that is adopted by most runners and promotes these remarkably high injury rates—are that it produces higher impact forces with the ground, greater forces at the knee with each impact, increased rates of force loading after impact, and dramatically augmented hip adduction (inward movement of the thigh during stance) compared with optimal form. As a reminder, optimal form features midfoot-striking with the foot closer to a point under the body's center of mass. The consequence of the elevated forces and greater hip adduction is a heightened risk of being injured at some point during the training year.

One of the key problems with heel-striking is that it increases an important variable called VALR—the vertical average loading rate of impact force. Research has shown that VALR is the strongest predictor of injury risk in runners; runners with higher values of VALR have greater risks of both bony and soft-tissue injuries (5). In effect, with heel-striking, the impact force experienced by the leg increases too quickly (VALR rises too rapidly), compared with midfoot-striking.

Hitting the ground heel first (as 95 percent of runners do), instead of a midfoot- or forefoot-landing, roughly doubles the risk of running-related injury (6). Heel-striking produces a dramatically higher initial spike in ground-reaction force, compared with forefoot- or midfoot- striking, which is another way of saying that VALR is increased in heel-strikers (figure 4.1) (7).

As can be seen in figure 4.1, one of the key challenges associated with heel-first collisions is that the loading rate of force applied to the leg upon landing is much higher with heel-striking. In other words, the rate of increase for the force felt by the leg is higher with heel-striking; the leg experiences the force more rapidly, with less time to react. Higher forces on the leg are linked with a greater risk of injury (8), and higher loading rates of force are also connected with a larger probability of getting hurt (5, 9). Runners who shift

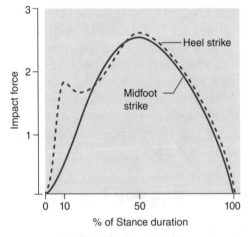

Figure 4.1 **Impact forces associated with heel- and midfoot-striking. Note: Just 10 percent of the way into stance the vertical impact force is nearly double for the heel-strike, compared with a midfoot-strike.**

from heel-striking to forefoot- or midfoot-landing significantly reduce the magnitude of impact force (10).

How do other aspects of form influence injury rate? Shank angle at initial ground contact (SAT), maximal shank angle (MSA), and Reversal of Sweep (ROS) are relatively new terms in the study of form, so few investigations have been conducted concerning their effects on injury rate. However, SAT and foot-strike pattern are strongly linked. The greater the SAT, the more likely it is that a runner is using a heel-strike ground-contact strategy. Thus, high SAT should be linked with lofty rates of impact-force loading.

The Role of Cadence

Considerable research has explored the link between another related running-form variable, cadence, and the risk of injury. A 2014 study conducted by Rachel Lenhart and her colleagues at the University of Wisconsin at Madison revealed that a 10 percent increase in cadence (step rate) during running reduced peak knee-joint force by 14 percent (11), an effect that should lower the chances of developing patello-femoral pain and knee injury. Previous work by the same group had demonstrated that a mere 5 percent increase in step rate diminished total work performed at the knee per step, reduced the extent of heel-strike at initial ground contact, diminished hip adduction during stance, and also lessened the internal rotation of the hip when the foot was on the ground (12). Stance is the portion of gait during which the foot is in contact with the ground and when it appears that the foot is going backward relative to the rest of the body. In reality, the body is moving forward over the foot, and stance occurs from the instant of initial ground contact to the moment of toe-off. Hip adduction is an inward (medially directed) movement of the thigh during stance. An increased hip adduction angle means that the thigh moves medially and more dramatically during stance, compared with normal hip adduction (figures 4.2 and 4.3).

These factors—reduced peak knee-joint force and lessened hip adduction and rotation—should diminish the risk of knee injury and another important malady called "iliotibial band syndrome" (ITBS). Runners with ITBS generally run with relatively slow cadences (less than 165 steps per minute) and display high degrees of hip adduction and rotation during stance.

While SAT was not measured in the two studies mentioned above, it is important to note that SAT and cadence are strongly linked. The average runner, for example, tends to run with an SAT of about 16 degrees and a cadence of approximately 160 to 164 steps per minute (13). A runner with a cadence of 180 steps per minute, however, often has an SAT of only six to 10 degrees (14). In the studies carried out by Heiderscheit and his colleagues, it is reasonable to assume that as cadence increased, SAT decreased concomitantly, heel-striking was less pronounced; and thus knee-joint forces, hip adduction, and hip rotation were reduced, decreasing the risk of injury.

Figure 4.2 Slower cadences are linked with greater adduction angles, which correspond with a greater risk of injury.

Figure 4.3 Among runners, research reveals that an increase in cadence is usually associated with a smaller hip adduction angle during stance.

Common Injuries and Common Form

Research has linked an increased risk of suffering a running-related injury with various form-related body alignment patterns, particularly those patterns displayed by the average runner. Three common running injuries—ITBS, tibial stress fractures, and patellofemoral pain syndrome (characterized by strong discomfort in the front of the knee)—have been linked with increased peak hip adduction angle during the stance phase of gait. The important form-related point here is that hip adduction angle is strongly associated not only with cadence, but also with an important variable called "heel-strike distance" (figure 4.4). This is simply the horizontal distance between the center of the pelvis and the heel at initial contact with the ground: the greater the heel-strike distance, the larger the hip adduction angle (15).

In general, heel-strike distance is a direct function of SAT; the greater the heel-strike distance, the higher the SAT. Thus there is a straightforward connection between SAT and the likelihood of injury. A large SAT leads to large heel-strike distances, which promotes hip adduction and injury.

The increased inward movement of the thigh associated with greater peak hip adduction angle places more stress on the iliotibial band on the lateral side of the thigh and the knee itself and thus can be a source of training-related knee discomfort. This can be addressed by reducing SAT and thus heel-strike distance. (Training techniques that promote a reduction in SAT are revealed in chapter 7.) In addition, appropriate, running-specific strength training can improve the strength of the iliotibial band in a functional way and thus reduce peak hip adduction angle, providing runners with further protection from iliotibial band syndrome and knee pain. (Running-specific strengthening techniques are discussed in chapter 14.) Excessive inward movement of the thigh during stance can be considered to be a breakdown in form, which increases the risk of injury.

Overall, an expanded heel-strike distance (and thus larger SAT), increased peak vertical ground reaction force, expanded peak hip adduction, and a decrease in knee flexion at

Figure 4.4 **Greater heel-strike distance is linked with higher hip adduction and an increased risk of injury.**

initial ground contact (a straighter leg) have been linked with patellofemoral pain (16) and a heightened risk of both iliotibial band syndrome (17) and tibial stress fracture (18) (figures 4.5 and 4.6).

Exercise scientists recently investigated whether just changing cadence could push these mechanics in the opposite direction, preventing injury. They wanted to determine if increased cadence would lead to shorter

Figure 4.5 **Research indicates that landing on the ground with a straight leg increases the risk of serious running injury.**

Figure 4.6 **Research indicates making contact with the ground with the leg flexed at the knee lowers the risk of injury.**

heel-strike distance and thus smaller SAT, reduced vertical ground reaction force, better control of the hip during stance, and a more highly flexed knee at impact with the ground (19). It would be rather magical if higher cadence could produce all of these positive results and would certainly reveal how important cadence is for optimal running form.

Cadence Retraining

The cadence research studied heel-strikers who were running about 19 miles a week with a slow cadence, averaging 164 steps per minute. All of the participants went through a six-week "cadence retraining intervention." To increase cadence, each runner trained (and matched their steps) with a metronome, set at a cadence 10 percent greater than the individual's preferred cadence (in this case, approximately 180 steps per minute). All of the participants completed at least 50 percent of weekly mileage with the cadence uplift of 10 percent (180 steps/minute). They were all guided by either the metronome or another audible tool, such as music with a tempo of 180 beats per minute or a metronome-like smart-phone application.

After six weeks of higher-cadence training, the runners had not raised their natural cadence to 180, but they had improved to about 170 steps per minute. This step-rate upgrade had a number of positive consequences. For example, at 170 steps per minute, the runners experienced a decrease in ankle dorsiflexion at initial ground contact (i.e., they had less-pronounced heel-strikes); their peak hip adduction angle was smaller; and the vertical loading rate of force on the leg was lessened. All of these differences are associated with a lower risk of developing three key running injuries: knee pain, stress fractures, and iliotibial band troubles.

This useful study not only revealed that a simple increase in cadence could produce better running mechanics, but also provided a simple mechanism for improving form for the average runner (by using a metronome set at a 10 percent higher cadence than usual). Using this technique, runners can improve their cadence significantly in a short period of time.

The inquiry also supports other research that has linked increased cadence with changes in gait, and, in turn, the changes in gait are positively linked with a decrease in overuse running injuries (20). Interestingly, the simple act of running barefoot tends to increase cadence and is linked with similar advancements in running mechanics, including a smaller SAT, diminished heel-strike distance, and a reduced reliance on heel-striking (21). More information about unshod running will be provided in chapter 12, and barefoot running will be utilized as a tool for improving form in the drills outlined in chapters 6 through 8.

Why does a simple form change such as increased cadence lead to better running mechanics? The quicker cadence tends to bring the foot back closer to the body for initial ground contact. This prevents heel-strike distance and

SAT from becoming too large and also shortens the braking phase of stance. Higher cadence also limits the extent of ankle dorsiflexion at initial ground contact (in other words, it minimizes heel-striking). Heel-striking is minimized because at a faster cadence, runners don't have time to land on the heel, then place the sole of the foot on the ground, and then move through stance to toe-off, as they are unable to maintain a higher cadence with all of this excess action (compared with landing toward the middle to front of the foot and "bouncing" forward).

With a higher cadence and midfoot- to forefoot-striking, the lower limb is placed in a more spring-like landing posture, with a less straight leg, a more highly flexed knee, and a more neutral or slightly plantar-flexed foot at contact with the ground. This allows better distribution of force through the leg after impact and slows down the peak loading rate of impact force through the leg.

When the foot is more closely aligned with the center of mass of the body, the hip tends to be in a more neutral position. It is not as flexed as it is with a large heel-strike distance and a big SAT. Thus, the muscles which control hip adduction (namely the gluteus medius and iliotibial band) have a greater mechanical advantage and are placed in a stronger position from the standpoint of controlling hip adduction. This is another reason why shorter heel-strike distance, smaller SAT, and higher cadence are all linked with better control of the thigh and knee, and thus lower hip adduction and a reduction in impact forces at the knee.

Cadence and SAT are naturally linked together: It is very difficult for a runner to have a high cadence if she has a big SAT. She also can't have a high cadence if ROS is too minimal because this elongates heel-strike distance and thus the time spent getting the body up and over the foot with each step, increasing the stance phase of gait and automatically slowing cadence. In the study in which runners practiced running with a cadence of 180 steps per minute, the increase in cadence resulted in a decrease in SAT; it is likely this decrease can be attributed to the reduction in heel-strike distance. Conversely, a training intervention that produces a reduced SAT should spontaneously raise cadence. Overall, it is clear that increases in cadence and ROS, and a decrease in SAT, should promote a lower risk of injury. Given the incredibly high injury rate among runners today, it is very important for running athletes to incorporate drills into their training that optimize cadence, ROS, and SAT.

That said, while a shift from heel- to midfoot- striking will certainly reduce stress on the heel, tibia, and knee—and most likely the frequency of heel pain, tibial stress fractures, knee discomfort, and ITBS—it also increases the work that must be performed by the non-heel portion of the foot and Achilles tendon with each step. This temporarily increases the risk of injury to those areas. Therefore, a heel-striking runner should not make a sudden and dramatic plunge into midfoot-landings. Rather, he should very gradually adjust to midfoot-striking over a period of many weeks.

This gradual adjustment can be accomplished by drilling, or using the midfoot-strike-enhancing drills described in chapter 6, on a daily basis. Over the course of many weeks, with daily drill employment, a runner's "drilling form" and spontaneously adopted running form will gradually approach each other and eventually unify in a way that strengthens the foot, Achilles tendon, and calf and does not produce abrupt increases in force and work output for those regions of the lower appendage.

Running Form and Performance

The best research to date linking changes in running form with actual race performances was carried out by Leena Paavolainen, Heikki Rusko, and others and their scientific team at the Research Institute for Olympic Sports in Jyväskylä, Finland (22, 23). In one investigation, Rusko and colleagues divided experienced endurance runners into two groups. The two collections of athletes were initially similar in ability and trained for the same number of hours (about nine per week over a nine-week period); but the "explosive" group devoted about three of those hours per week to explosive training consisting of short sprints, jumping exercises, hurdling, quick-action leg presses, and high-velocity hamstring curls. In contrast, the control group spent just 15 minutes per week engaged in such activities, instead engaging in larger amounts of traditional endurance training (including steady running at moderate paces).

The control group improved maximal aerobic capacity ($\dot{V}O_2$max) after nine weeks of training, but they were not able to upgrade 5K performance. In contrast, the explosive group failed to advance $\dot{V}O_2$max but sped up their 5K times by about 30 seconds (a compromise that most runners would be willing to make). There were a number of positive changes achieved by the explosive group over the course of the study, including enhanced running economy; heightened maximal speed (measured during an all-out 20-meter sprint); advanced explosiveness during jumping tests; and an upswing in a variable called VMART—the highest velocity attained during a maximal, anaerobic running test on the treadmill. VMART reflects the ability to carry out progressively faster running intervals for a longer time during a challenging workout, or in other words, the development of greater fatigue resistance during high-speed running.

Improvements in running economy and VMART were significantly correlated with better 5K performance. Changes in VMART were strongly linked with decreased contact time, or a shortening of the duration of stance. The stance phase of gait was diminished by about 10 milliseconds per step in the explosive group, which undoubtedly seems small to the casual observer. However, those 10 milliseconds represent extra time "glued to the ground" during running and thus time lost to forward movement. These additional milliseconds add up over the course of a race. To summarize, Rusko's runners used explosive training to decrease stance duration and thereby increase cadence, a key form and performance variable; therefore, they were able to shave 30 seconds from their 5K performances.

The Three Phases of Stance

It is important to note that the stance phase of gait can be divided into three parts:

1. The braking phase, when the foot has just made contact with the ground and horizontal braking forces are being produced
2. The vertical propulsion phase, when the forces applied to the ground are directed in a vertical direction
3. The horizontal propulsive phase, when the foot's interaction with the ground produces forward horizontal forces and the runner's body is propelled forward

Explosive training shortens stance time. Most likely it enhances nervous system responsiveness. This allows a quicker passage through the three components of stance without diminishing horizontal and vertical propulsive forces; it therefore shortens stance in a positive way.

In the second inquiry (24), Rusko and colleagues asked 17 male endurance athletes to take part in a 5K time trial and also undertake a variety of tests of running capacity (including an evaluation of running economy and an all-out 20-meter sprint). They found that 5K performance was significantly associated with 20-meter sprint speed and also with ground-contact time (stance duration) and cadence measured during the 20-meter blast. The higher the cadence and shorter the stance duration during 20-meter sprinting, the faster the 5K.

Foot-strike pattern is also linked with performance. Research has found that faster endurance performers tend to use the midfoot and forefoot ground-contact strategies, while slower runners are more likely to be heel-strikers (25). Anecdotal observations also support the connection between higher-level performance and both midfoot-landing and smaller SAT. For example, elite Kenyan endurance runners tend to run with

Getty Images/Joshua Blanchard

Figure 4.7   American elite runner Desiree Davila Linden employs a pronounced heel-strike landing pattern and an SAT of greater than 10 degrees when she runs the marathon.

Figure 4.8   Kenyan elite runner Mary Wangui employs a midfoot-strike pattern and an SAT of ~ 6 degrees when she runs.

an SAT of between zero and six degrees, while elite American runners often run with an SAT greater than six degrees. Furthermore, elite Kenyans tend to be midfoot-strikers, while American elites tend to collide with the ground heel first (figures 4.7 and 4.8).

A check of recent top performances in the world for 2016 reveals that for the 10K (road racing) there are 24 elite male Kenyans in the top 30 and no elite American males. On the women's side, for the 10K there are 18 elite Kenyans (including two under the author's management) and only two elite Americans. For the marathon, there are 19 Kenyan men and zero American males in the top 30, and there are eight Kenyan women and zero American females. It is unlikely that the reduced SAT and more pronounced midfoot-landings at touchdown of the Kenyan runners play no role at all in their superiority over American runners. Simply put, great form leads to great performances.

Running Form and Running Economy

Running economy is the oxygen cost of running at a specific speed, and it is strongly linked with endurance performance. In general, the lower the oxygen cost of running at competitive velocities, the faster the performance (26). Just as shorter-duration stance was linked with higher performance in the Rusko research, it is also tightly connected with enhanced running economy (27, 28). Of course, shorter stance time is associated with a smaller SAT and with midfoot-striking, as opposed to heel-striking. These key form variables appear to be directly linked with running economy.

Summary

The running form you choose can either increase or decrease your risk of injury. Deciding to run with a large shank angle at ground contact, a straight leg at ground contact, a heel-strike ground-contact pattern, a relative absence of sweep, or a moderate to low cadence increases the risk of getting hurt.

In contrast, running with an SAT of approximately six to seven degrees, with a flexed knee at initial ground contact, a midfoot- to forefoot-strike pattern, an ROS of about 70 percent of maximal shank angle, and a cadence of 180 or more lowers the chances of injury.

Those factors that advance the risk of injury also harm performance because they are associated with longer stance phases of gait, greater braking forces during stance, and lower cadences. It should be mentioned, too, that injury harms performance by thwarting a key producer of outstanding performance times: consistent training.

Those form factors which decrease the risk of injury are great for performance because they increase cadence, reduce the duration of stance, limit braking effects, and promote the production of maximum propulsive forces during the optimal stage of stance.

References

1. Running USA: Statistics, http://www.runningusa.org/statistics (accessed 2014).

2. Ibid.

3. C.A. Macera et al., "Predicting Lower-Extremity Injuries Among Habitual Runners," *Archives of Internal Medicine* 149, no. 11 (1989): 2565–2568.

4. B. Heiderscheit, "Always on the Run," *Journal of Orthopaedic Sports Physical Therapy* 44, no. 10 (2014): 724–726.

5. I. Davis et al, "Greater Vertical Impact Loading in Female Runners with Medically Diagnosed Injuries: A Prospective Investigation," http://bjsm.bmj.com/ (accessed 2016).

6. A.I. Daoud et al., "Foot Strike and Injury Rates in Endurance Runners: A Retrospective Study," *Medicine & Science in Sports and Exercise* 44, no. 7 (2012): 1325–1334.

7. Ibid.

8. C.E. Milner et al., "Biomechanical Factors Associated With Tibial Stress Fracture in Female Runners," *Medicine & Science in Sports and Exercise* 38 (2006): 323–328.

9. M.B. Schaffler, E.L. Radin, and D.B. Burr, "Mechanical and Morphological Effects of Strain Rate on Fatigue of Compact Bone," *Bone* 10, no. 3 (1989): 207–214.

10. Y. Shih, K.L. Lin, and T.Y. Shiang, "Is the Foot Striking Pattern More Important Than Barefoot or Shod Conditions in Running?" *Gait Posture* 38, no. 3 (2013): 490–494.

11. R.L. Lenhart et al., "Increasing Running Step Rate Reduces Patellofemoral Joint Forces," *Medicine & Science in Sports and Exercise* 46, no. 3 (2014): 557–564.

12. B. Heiderscheit et al., "The Effects of Step Rate Manipulation on Joint Mechanics During Running," *Medicine & Science in Sports and Exercise* 42, no. 2 (2011): 296–302.

13. Walter Reynolds, personal communication, June 6, 2017.

14. Ibid.

15. J.F. Hafer et al., "The Effect of a Cadence Retraining Protocol on Running Biomechanics and Efficiency: A Pilot Study," *Journal of Sports Sciences* 33, no. 7 (2014): 1–8.

16. J.D. Willson and I.S. Davis, "Lower Extremity Mechanics of Females With and Without Patellofemoral Pain Across Activities With Progressively Greater Task Demands," *Clinical Biomechanics* 23, no. 2 (2008): 203–211.

17. B. Noehren, I. Davis, and J. Hamill, "Prospective Study of the Biomechanical Factors Associated With Iliotibial Band Syndrome," *Clinical Biomechanics,* 27, no. 4 (2007): 366–371.

18. M.B. Pohl et al., "Biomechanical Predictors of Retrospective Tibial Stress Fractures in Runners," *Journal of Biomechanics* 41, no. 6 (2008): 1160–1165.

19. J.F. Hafer, "The Effect of a Cadence Retraining Protocol on Running Biomechanics and Efficiency: A Pilot Study," *Journal of Sports Sciences* 33, no. 7(2015): 724–731.

20. B.C. Heiderscheit, "Effects of Step Rate Manipulation on Joint Mechanics During Running," *Medicine & Science in Sports and Exercise,* 43 no. 2 (2011): 296–302.

21. R. Squadrone, and C. Gallozzi, "Biomechanical and Physiological Comparison of Barefoot and Two Shod Conditions in Experienced Barefoot Runners," *The Journal of Sports Medicine and Physical Fitness* 49, no. 1 (2009): 6–13.

22. L. Paavolainen et al., "Explosive-Strength Training Improves 5-km Running Time by Improving Running Economy and Muscle Power," *Journal of Applied Physiology* 86, no. 5 (1999): 1527–1533.

23. L.M. Paavolainen, A.T. Nummela, and H.T. Rusko, "Neuromuscular Characteristics and Muscle Power as Determinants of 5-km Running Performance," *Medicine & Science in Sports and Exercise* 31, no. 1 (1999): 124–130.

24. Ibid.

25. H. Hasegawa, T. Yamauchi, and W.J. Kraemer, "Foot Strike Patterns of Runners at the 15-km Point During an Elite-Level Half Marathon," *Journal of Strength & Conditioning Research* 21, no. 3 (2007): 888–893.

26. K.R. Barnes and A.E. Kilding, "Strategies to Improve Running Economy," *Sports Medicine* 45, no. 1 (2015): 37–56.

27. J. Santos-Concejero et al., "Influence of the Biomechanical Variables of the Gait Cycle in Running Economy," *International Journal of Sport Science* 36 (2014): 95–108.

28. J. Santos-Concejero et al., "Differences in Ground Contact Time Explain the Less Efficient Running Economy in North African Runners," *Biol. Sport* 30 (2013): 181–187.

PART

II

Assessing and Improving Form

5

Assessing Form

Six key elements of form assessment represent the biggest influencers of performance, running economy, and risk of injury. Therefore, these six should be measured carefully via video analysis:

1. Determination of how far ahead of the body the leg moves during the swing phase of gait and thus calculation of maximum shank angle (MSA)
2. Measurement of reversal of swing (ROS), or how far back the shank and foot move from MSA before hitting the ground
3. Determination of the ROS-to-MSA ratio (ROS/MSA)
4. Measurement of the shank angle at initial impact with the ground (SAT, or shank angle at touchdown)
5. Determination of the foot angle at touchdown (FAT)
6. Confirmation of posture

A smartphone with video capabilities or a video camera are necessary to carry out the video analysis. The brand of the device does not matter, but the video instrument must be capable of recording at a rate of no less than 240 fps (frames per second).

Bear in mind that it is critical to determine MSA, ROS, SAT, and FAT with great precision. If you cannot determine exactly when a runner's foot strikes the ground, for example, you will not be able to assess SAT and FAT accurately.

Take the case of a runner moving along with a cadence of 180 steps per minute (three steps per second). As she runs, the goal is to "see" the exact moment when each foot makes contact with the ground—the precise instant when the stance phase of gait begins and SAT and FAT can be measured.

Imagine what might happen if the video device were taking images at only 30 frames per second: That would mean an image would be captured every 1000/30 = 33.33 milliseconds.

That may seem like plenty of footage. But when a video device captures only 30 frames per second, it will be impossible to tell if the first frame showing the foot touching the ground represents initial impact, or if it shows the foot after it has been on the ground for a number of milliseconds. In the intervening milliseconds after the true initial impact, the runner's body may have moved significantly ahead over the foot, and thus the shank angle might have changed significantly. In other words, the measured SAT would be wrong.

Now, imagine this same scenario with a video device recording at 240 Hz. Instead of 33 milliseconds between images, there are now 1000/240 = approximately 4 milliseconds between images. On average, when estimating SAT, the video analysis will be off by about two milliseconds per frame, compared with about 16 milliseconds per frame for a 30 Hz recording. The degree of accuracy at 240 fps is simply much greater.

Taking Video Footage

To carry out the form assessment, try to find a location where the runner being analyzed can run freely on flat ground for 60 meters or so. In a trial run, position yourself at the midway point, far enough away from the runner so that you can capture the runner's entire body as he runs by you. The runner will be moving from left to right (or right to left), so that you are taking a lateral view as he runs. Make certain that you are in a position so that you can capture two steps (right and left) as he moves by. Verify this by having him run past and then checking out the video you have taken. The maximum observed number of steps should be three. If you are getting four steps, you are standing too far away from the runner.

Have the runner begin at one end of the 60-meter running surface and run past you in a very natural way. Emphasize to the runner that he should relax and run with his normal pattern of movement. After the runner has warmed up thoroughly, have him run past you at a very easy pace. Take video as he moves past, from right to left or left to right. Again, verify that the video has been recorded properly and that you have captured at least two steps. Save the video for follow-up analysis.

Repeat this process two more times: once at a moderate pace (around marathon tempo if possible or at least a little slower than a 10K-race speed), and then again at a fast velocity (5K pace or faster for a distance runner and 1500-meter speed or quicker for a middle-distance competitor). Review the three videos and make sure that they have been recorded properly, with two or three observed ground contacts per video.

Check the quality of the images, specifically the sharpness of the views of the feet making impact with the ground. If the feet seem rather small in the video or are not in focus, retake the three videos while standing closer to the runner as he passes.

You are now ready to begin the analysis.

Analyzing the Video

You can learn a lot by simply watching the videos you have taken, especially in slow motion. However, you will need an app to properly analyze the videos you have created and to precisely determine posture and four key variables: MSA, ROS, SAT, and FAT. There are several different apps on the market, but a highly functional one is Coach's Eye by TechSmith. Coach's Eye provides slow-motion analysis and a variety of useful form-measurement tools. The app allows users to easily share any video (email or upload) with another party, such as a coach, coaching client, or running partner. The app is also inexpensive (in fact, the basic app is free), especially considering the wealth of form information it can provide. If you intend to obtain Coach's Eye or a similar app, be sure to purchase the "angle-measurement" tool as well. This is also inexpensive and is indispensable for measuring MSA, ROS (and thus ROS/MSA), SAT, FAT, and posture.

Once you have your chosen app installed on your smart phone, you are ready to complete the analysis. Begin with the first video taken at a slow run. Open the video with Coach's Eye or a similar app and roll it through manually—frame by frame—until you are certain that you are seeing the maximum forward swing of one leg (right or left, whichever swings forward first in the video). Toggle the video back and forth until you are sure that you have the max swing point and thus MSA.

Once you are confident that you are seeing the maximum forward swing of the leg, you are ready to measure maximum shank angle (MSA). Using the frame which displays max forward swing, and with the additional angle tool you downloaded, draw a straight line from the center of the athlete's knee,

Here are the four leading video-analysis apps to consider purchasing:

1. Coach's Eye (TechSmith): www.coachseye.com/
2. Hudl Technique (formerly known as UberSense which was acquired by Hudl in 2014): www.hudl.com/products/technique
3. Dartfish Express (Dartfish): www.dartfish.com/Mobile
4. ReplayCam (DreamGarage Inc.): https://itunes.apple.com/us/app/replaycam-the-time-shift-video-camera/id590197399?mt=8

Here is a link to a comparison review of the first three: http://crosscountryskitechnique.com/review-top-3-sport-video-analysis-apps/

down the lower part of the leg, and through the foot. Make sure that this line runs straight through the middle of the lower part of the leg—don't let it "pull away" from the leg (figure 5.1). You can end this line slightly below the foot, but be certain that the line is straight and travels down the middle of the lower limb from knee to foot.

Now you are ready to draw the second line, the one that will allow the measurement of MSA. From the bottom of the first line, draw this second line straight forward, parallel with the ground. The two lines you have drawn will meet just below the foot and will form an angle between them (figure 5.2). The app's angle tool allows you to measure this angle automatically.

Now MSA can be determined: It is simply the angle you have just measured minus 90 degrees. For example, in this case the measurement of the

Figure 5.1   **Begin by drawing a straight line through the shank.**

Figure 5.2   **Draw a second line which starts at the bottom of the first line and extends straight and parallel with the ground.**

shank at its furthest position forward yielded an angle of 111 degrees, which is very common, and the maximum shank angle is $111 - 90 = 21$ degrees.

Measuring Shank Angle at Impact

After determining MSA, you can ascertain the all-important shank angle at touchdown (SAT). Continue toggling the video forward frame by frame until you reach what appears to be the first impact with the ground.

Once you have settled on the video frame associated with initial impact, again use your app to draw a straight line from the knee, down through the lower part of the leg, and through the foot. Make sure this line stays in the exact center of the lower portion of the leg at all times (as you did when measuring MSA). End this line just below the foot (figure 5.3).

Then draw a second line that begins at the lowest point of the first line and extends straight forward, parallel with the ground. Once this second line is drawn, you will have formed a nice angle. The app will automatically indicate the size of the angle. Subtract 90 degrees from the measured angle, and the result will be the SAT.

In this case, the two lines at the moment of impact produce an angle of 108 degrees (figure 5.4). As shown in the equation $108 - 90 = 18$ degrees. An SAT of 18 degrees sounds quite high but is actually very common. Unfortunately, an 18-degree SAT is usually associated with a relatively straight leg at impact with the ground—a key running-form flaw that produces elevated impact forces and thus a greater risk of injury plus higher braking forces and thus a throttling effect on speed.

Figure 5.3 Once you have found the exact moment of foot strike, draw a line straight through the middle of the shank through the foot to the ground.

Figure 5.4 **SAT is measured with two lines, one running straight down the middle of the shank and the other originating at the base of the first line and running parallel with the ground.**

Measuring How FAT Your Landing Is

You are now ready to measure foot angle at touchdown (FAT). From that same point of initial contact with the ground (the instant where you measured SAT), draw a line straight through the foot, from the base of the heel, through the bottoms of the toes (or through the corresponding parts of the running shoe). Draw a second line that originates from the point of contact with the ground (at the heel or front of the foot), parallel with the ground (figure 5.5). The resulting angle is the FAT. If the ankle is dorsiflexed at the moment of initial contact, FAT will be positive. If the ankle is plantar-flexed at touchdown, FAT will be negative (figures 5.6).

Finally, measure MSA, SAT, and FAT for the other leg; then repeat these measurements for the videos taken at moderate and high speeds. Record all of the angles in table form (table 5.1). All of these angles will be essential as you begin the process of upgrading running form.

Figure 5.5 To determine FAT, first draw a line straight through the foot, from the base of the heel through the bottoms of the toes. Next, draw a second line parallel with the ground, beginning at the heel. If the ankle is dorsi-flexed at the moment of contact, FAT will be positive.

Figure 5.6 To determine FAT when the ankle is plantar-flexed at touchdown, first draw a line straight through the foot, from the bottoms of the toes through the base of the heel. Next, draw a second line parallel with the ground, beginning at the toes. If the ankle is plan-tar-flexed at the moment of contact, FAT will be negative.

TABLE 5.1

Form Variables for Right and Left Legs

MEASUREMENTS	RIGHT LEG	LEFT LEG
MSA		
SAT		
ROS		
ROS/MSA ratio		
FAT		

From Anderson, 2018, *Running Form: How to Run Faster and Prevent Injury*, (Champaign, IL: Human Kinetics).

Calculating ROS and the ROS/MSA Ratio

As mentioned, to measure reversal of swing (ROS) simply subtract SAT from MSA (ROS = MSA – SAT). For example, if MSA is 18 degrees and SAT is 12 degrees, then ROS is 18 – 12 = 6 degrees. Determine ROS for both legs at all three running speeds and include it in table 5.1.

Calculation of the all-important ROS/MSA ratio is similarly simple: Just divide ROS by the MSA. In the case above, 6/18 yields an ROS/MSA ratio of .33. Looking at this another way, we can say that after attaining her MSA, the runner swept the foot back 33 percent of the way before hitting the ground (or reversed swing by 33 percent). This is a critically important number to know, since small ROS/MSA ratios are associated with imparting little kinetic energy to the ground, and extra-large ratios, although rare, may put the leg in a disadvantageous position from the standpoint of producing optimal propulsive forces. An optimal ROS/MSA ratio is about .7 to .75.

Comparing the Three Videos

The table that you have generated (table 5.1) provides tremendous insight into your current form. As you develop better form over time, you will produce new tables and will be able to monitor your form improvements in an objective, quantitative way.

You will also likely find that the numbers are quite different between your right leg and left leg. While this might seem surprising, it is completely normal: Very few runners have legs that function identically. Most runners—even Usain Bolt—have a fast leg and a slow leg, where one leg does a better job of optimizing the form variables. From the standpoints of performance improvement and injury prevention, this is actually a very good (not disappointing) thing to know. You now have the concepts of good form and the quantitative tools you need to work diligently on both legs, with special focus paid to your slow leg.

You may find that your right leg commonly produces an SAT of six to eight degrees, while your left is consistently at 2 degrees (figures 5.9 and 5.10). When you carry out your form drills, you can concentrate more intently on the left leg to bring it in line with the right. A similar situation may prevail with MSA, ROS, and FAT; but with video analysis and proper drilling, you can get the legs functioning optimally and in nearly identical fashion.

Setting Form Goals

Unless you already have optimal form, your work is now set out for you. If you are a distance runner, optimal SAT is around five to seven degrees, and ROS/MSA is approximately .7 to .75. These are the values that you should

Figure 5.9 This elite runner has an SAT of 8 degrees with her right leg.

Figure 5.10 However, with her left leg SAT is 2 degrees. By using the drills found in this book, she can equalize SAT at ~6 degrees in each leg.

strive to achieve, using the form-enhancing drills and techniques described in the following chapters. You will also incorporate drills into training to establish a neutral or slightly negative FAT. Please note that MSA actually increases with running speed—the higher the speed, the greater the MSA. However, optimal SAT and ROS/MSA ratio do NOT change with running speed—they remain at 6 to 7 degrees and .7 to .75, respectively.

If you are a sprinter, three of the optimal values are quite different: FAT will be more negative, as the ankle will be more plantar-flexed at touch-down and initial contact will be with the front of the foot. MSA may be as great as 34 degrees and ROS may be as high as 26 to 28 degrees, in order to produce the greater speeds required for sprinting. However, SAT will still be approximately six to seven degrees.

Measuring Posture

To assess posture, select a moment from the video when the athlete is in mid-stance, and use the app to position three points on the runner's body: center of the hip, center of the thorax, and middle of the head. Then draw a straight line from the hip to the center of the thorax, and another straight line from the thorax to the middle of the head.

When posture is good, the two lines should be continuous—that is, the thorax point should appear on the straight line drawn from the hip to the head. More commonly, the line from the thorax to the skull is inclined for-ward, compared with the line from the hip to the chest, and this can produce form trouble that hurts performance (figure 5.11).

The ideal complete straight line, which includes all three points (hip, trunk, and head), should have a slight forward inclination (figure 5.12). Don't be confused by this. It is bad when the upper line from the trunk to

Figure 5.11   **With poor posture, two distinct lines are created, one from the hips to the thorax, and one from thorax to center of head.**

Figure 5.12   **With good posture, a line through the center of the hips, center of thorax, and center of head is a straight line with a slightly forward overall inclination.**

the head is inclined forward relative to the lower line (from the trunk to the hip). But it is very good when the two lines make one straight line and that whole line is leaning forward. This helps the body move forward, rather than merely upward as propulsive force is applied to the ground during the stance phase of gait.

As posture can be somewhat fluid, determine posture during various phases of stance and swing for each leg at all three speeds. Take note of any differences between legs or any dramatic changes in posture over the course of the gait cycle. Drills and techniques for improving posture will be described fully in chapter 10.

Summary

You now have all the skills and tools you need to assess your running form properly. You can determine posture, foot-strike pattern (FAT), maximum shank angle (MSA), reversal of swing (ROS), shank angle at impact (SAT), and the key ratio, ROS/MSA, in straightforward ways. In the following chapters, you will learn exactly how to optimize your form and become a more-economical, faster runner with a lower risk of injury.

6

Improving Foot-Strike Pattern

It takes just a few seconds during form drills to transform from a heel-striker to a midfoot-striker. However, the total transformation—to the point at which all running is completed with a midfoot-striking pattern—can take several months.

The reason for the extensive transformation period is not that it takes a long time to learn how to hit the ground midfooted. As mentioned, most heel-striking runners can develop a midfoot-strike pattern nearly instantly, when instructed to do so. However, heel-striking runners won't necessarily preserve the midfoot-strikes when they move from drills to actual training. In fact, they will usually fall back into their familiar heel-striking pattern. Most runners' neuromuscular systems are not eager to make sudden changes in form, even when they have the capacity to do so.

In this case, the stubbornness of the neuromuscular system is a good thing. Why shouldn't the heel-striking runner become a midfoot-striking zealot and instantly be saved from heel-strike peril? The basic problem is that shifting from heel-striking to midfoot-striking is wonderful in the long term (as it improves performance, enhances economy, and reduces the risk of injury); but it can produce physical problems in the short term if the shift is too abrupt.

As a runner moves along in heel-striking mode, each collision with the ground causes impact forces to pass directly through the heel, up the leg, and through the knee at a very high rate. The knee and hip areas in particular must carry out a lofty level of work to withstand, control, and react to these rapidly applied forces. In addition, the shin muscles are highly stressed, because they control the "slap-down" of the foot on the ground (ankle plantar-flexion) which occurs immediately after a heel-strike and which places great strain on the shin muscles and tendons. Only moderate pressure is placed on the calf muscles and Achilles tendon during heel-striking.

With midfoot-strikes, the force patterns change dramatically. Each impact with the ground immediately distributes forces throughout the foot and ankle. Because the runner is landing on the middle of the foot, there is no slap-down action (plantar flexion) of the ankle and foot. Instead, the ankle begins to undergo dorsiflexion immediately after impact, with the top of the foot moving closer to the shin instead of away from it. This places extra strain on the Achilles tendon and calf muscle complex (gastrocnemius and soleus), which must work together to prevent excessive dorsiflexion approximately 90 times per minute per ankle (assuming a decent cadence of 180 steps per minute).

It is not bad to ask the Achilles tendon and calf muscles to engage in more work per step with midfoot-striking. But if you have been a heel-striker, this will be new, and the introduction of new forces when running can result in problems with the muscles and connective tissues, especially when those forces are repeated 5,400 times per leg over the course of a one-hour run. This explains why traditional heel-strikers who don a pair of minimal shoes (or become sudden converts to barefoot running) and then go out for a 60-minute run often wake up the following morning with their calves as taut as suspension-bridge steel cables, sending a very doleful message of pain to the brain. Each calf was simply not ready to be insulted more than 5,000 times after basically sleeping through months and even years of heel-striking workouts. The mechanism for malady here is that a change from traditional, high-heeled running shoes to minimal shoes with little heel elevation usually changes form, pushing the runner naturally toward midfoot-striking.

The Perils of Too Much, Too Soon

This pitfall during the change from heel- to midfoot-striking partially explains what happened several years ago when, following the publication of a book that championed unshod-running, *Born to Run*, countless runners hit the streets and trails with absolutely nothing on their feet (1). The result was an epidemic of Achilles tendonitis, calf pain, calf-complex tightness, and even inflammation and stress reactions in the metatarsal bones of the feet which forced many runners to conclude that barefoot running was not even close to the magical activity described in the top-selling book (figure 6.1).

The difficulty, of course, was not with barefoot running per se (or even with the increased reliance on midfoot-striking), but rather with the too-rapid transition from shod to unshod running (and thus from heel- to midfoot-striking). Changes in form and alterations in training always require a slow and careful approach if a runner has any interest in minimizing the risk of injury. A more careful transition involves a very gradual immersion into the world of midfoot-striking, rather than the abrupt insertion of a challenging 60-minute run (with all impacts on the middle of the feet) into the training program.

One of the criticisms of the midfoot-landing strategy is that it simply changes the "hot points" in the leg (where impact forces are felt to the greatest extent and more work is carried out per step) and shifts the locus of potential injury from common heel-strike injury areas such as the heel, shin, knee, and hip to possible midfoot-strike injury areas such as the Achilles tendon, calf, and metatarsals of the foot. Studies in which participants quickly shift from heel-striking to midfoot-striking tend to support this contention. It is true that if you put a group of heel-striking runners on a program of midfoot- striking and enforce those midfoot-landings to the exclusion of the usual heel-strikes, most of the runners will be injured in a relatively short period of time. Further, most of those injuries will occur in the back of the lower part of the leg and also in the metatarsal bones of the feet, which are replacing the heels as "initial impact acceptors" during the first moments of stance. However, the conclusion that midfoot-striking is linked with a high rate of injury is not correct.

Figure 6.1 While shifting to unshod running does improve form and enhance running economy, if carried out too abruptly it can also lead to temporary problems in the calf, Achilles tendon, and even the metatarsal bones of the foot.

If an individual who has never performed biceps curls suddenly completes 100 reps of biceps curling with significantly heavy dumbbells and suffers from agonizingly painful biceps muscles the following day, should we conclude that bicep curls automatically produce injuries? No, it would be more realistic to conclude that the amount of curling—not the curling itself—led to the pain. Whether an injury will occur is determined by the amount of training, the underlying strength of the muscles and connective tissues involved in the activity, and the magnitude and loading rate of impact forces.

And that is why heel-striking is in such trouble when it comes to the injury argument. With heel-striking, the rate of loading of impact force within the leg is significantly higher, compared with midfoot-striking (refer to figure 2.3). This means that the muscles and connective tissues have less time to react to the forces to which they are exposed with each collision with the ground. The time to initial peak impact force is much shorter with heel-striking, compared with midfoot-strikes.

If this concept is confusing, think of it this way: Would you rather be struck with a hammer suddenly on the bottom of your tibia (your main shin bone) with a force equal to three times your body weight, or would you prefer to have that kind of force gradually applied to your tibia? The hammer blow is like heel-striking, and the gradual application of force is like midfoot-striking (remember that impact force travels up the leg much more rapidly with heel-striking).

Another key point to bear in mind is that the heel-striking runner usually hits the ground with a relatively straight leg, with the landing foot well in front of the body. By contrast, the midfoot-striker hits the ground with the foot closer to the body and the body's center of mass, and with the knee in a softer, more-flexed position compared to heel-strikers.

Which mode provides a softer landing, with less impact force travelling up the leg at high speed? Heel-striking is like ramming a hard pole into the ground at high speed, while midfoot-striking is like landing on a responsive spring (with ankle dorsi-flexion and knee flexion providing the springiness).

If you still believe that midfoot-striking is associated with a similar or even greater injury rate, compared with heel-striking, consider this scenario: Imagine you are standing on a high curb, about 24 inches high, above a cement roadway. You are going to jump down onto the road, and you must land on one foot (as you do when running). Would you rather make your landing on your heel with a straight, hard leg, or would you prefer to land midfooted with your knee flexed and your ankle ready to dorsi-flex to absorb the impact shock? Which plan carries the greater risk of injury? Do you still want to be a heel-striker when you run?

Drills for Transitioning to Midfoot-Striking

What follows here are drills that will help you make the transition from heel- to midfoot-striking. Please note that the initial drills should be carried out barefooted in order to provide superior proprioception and therefore a better feeling for midfoot-striking. This will help you sustain midfoot-strikes during your training and races, when you are wearing shoes. All drill durations are measured in minutes, and all should be performed with soft, flexed knees.

PHASE ONE: BAREFOOT

Activity	Duration (minutes)
Walk in place with midfoot-landings	1:00
Jog in place with midfoot-landings	4 × 1:00, with a short break in between each minute

Both the walking and jogging in place must be completed with a cadence of 180 steps per minute (190 if you are an elite athlete); use a runner's metronome or metronome app on your smart phone to verify. Conduct these drills before the main portion of your overall workout. Complete the drills about five times over the course of one week, or until you are completely certain that you can carry out both activities with midfoot-landings. You are then ready to move on to Phase Two.

Very important: As you are jogging in place, make sure that you make initial contact with the ground in the middle portion of the foot, with the heel striking the ground very shortly after this midfoot-strike (yes, the heel hits the ground on each step, but only after the midfoot region has "touched down.")

PHASE TWO: IN RUNNING SHOES

Activity	Duration (minutes)
Walk in place with midfoot-landings	1:00
Jog in place with midfoot-landings	4 × 1:00, with a short break in between each minute

Both activities must be completed with a cadence of 180 steps per minute (190 steps per minute if you are an elite athlete); use a runner's metronome or metronome app on your smart phone to verify. Complete the drills about five times over the course of one week, or until you are completely certain that you can carry out both activities with midfoot-landings while shod. You are then ready to move on to Phase Three.

Very important: As you are jogging in place, make sure that you make initial contact with the ground in the middle portion of the foot, with the heel striking the ground very shortly after this midfoot-strike (yes, the heel hits the ground on each step, but only after the midfoot region has "touched down.")

PHASE THREE: BAREFOOT

Activity	Duration (minutes)
Jog in place with midfoot-landings	1:00
Jog forward with midfoot-landings while taking "baby steps"	4 × 1:00, with a short break in between each minute

Both activities must be completed with a cadence of 180 steps per minute (190 steps per minute if you are an elite athlete); use a runner's metronome or metronome app on your smart phone to verify. Complete the drills about five times over the course of one week, or until you are completely certain that you can carry out both activities with midfoot landings while barefoot. You are then ready to move on to Phase Four.

Very important: As you are jogging forward with baby steps, make sure that you make initial contact with the ground in the middle portion of the foot, with the heel striking the ground very shortly after this midfoot strike (the heel hits the ground on each step, but only after the midfoot region has "touched down.")

PHASE FOUR: IN RUNNING SHOES

Activity	Duration (minutes)
Jog in place with midfoot- landings	1:00
Jog forward with midfoot-landings while taking "baby steps"	4 × 1:00, with short break in between each minute

Both activities should be completed with a cadence of 180 steps per minute (190 steps per minute if you are an elite athlete); use a runner's metronome or metronome app on your smart phone to verify. Complete the drills about five times over the course of one week, or until you are completely certain that you can carry out both activities with midfoot-landings while shod in your regular training or racing shoes (verify with video analysis, if possible). You are then ready to move on to the slightly more complicated drills in Phase Five.

Very important: As you are jogging forward with baby steps in shoes, make sure that you make initial contact with the ground in the middle portion of the foot, with the heel striking the ground very shortly after this midfoot-strike (the heel hits the ground on each step, but only after the midfoot region has "touched down.")

PHASE FIVE: IN RUNNING SHOES

Drill	Distance	Duration	Repetition
1	200 meters	120 seconds	1 time
2	200 meters	90 seconds	1 time
3	200 meters	60 seconds	1 time
4	200 meters	45 seconds	2 times
5	200 meters	30 seconds	2 times

Note: All drills use a midfoot-strike pattern. Cadence should be 180 steps per minute for non-elite runners (190 if elite); verify cadence with a metronome. Verify midfoot-striking with a video-analysis app, if possible.

Courtesy of Walt Reynolds, NovaSport Athlete Development.

Note for Phase Five: If for any phase you cannot sustain midfoot-striking at the specific, recommended pace, do *not* continue to the next drill. For example, if during Phase Four from above you find that you are reverting to heel-striking or are not able to maintain the pace, do not attempt to continue on to the final Phase Five. Instead, continue working on Phase Four, perhaps on a subsequent training day, until midfoot-striking can be maintained at the required cadence and running pace.

A common observation is that once runners have mastered midfoot-striking in drills, they often revert to heel-striking when they compete or carry out fast running in training. The work in Phase Five teaches a runner to utilize midfoot- striking, even at high velocities.

Please note: The form drills are put together in a way that makes them part of a very effective warm-up before a training session or competition. If the drills are conducted before a workout, proceed directly from the drills right into the training session; within the workout, *gradually* introduce more and more midfoot-striking over an extended period of time (the gradual inclusion of midfoot-striking lowers the risk of injury to your foot, Achilles tendon, and calf). For example, during the first week of drills you may want to focus on running with midfoot-strikes for about 10 percent of your normal training period (whatever you do after the drills are completed); the rest of the time, simply run with your customary form. During the second week of drills, transition to running with deliberate midfoot-striking for around 20 percent of your training time, and so on.

Contrast Runs

A couple of times per week, after an adequate warm-up, supplement the drills in this chapter with contrast runs, as follows:

1. Run at a moderate speed and a cadence of 180 steps per minute for approximately 50 meters with straight, hard legs, with little knee flexion at ground contact.

2. Rest for a few moments, and then run 50 meters at a moderate speed with a cadence of 180 steps per minute, with soft, slightly flexed knees at ground contact.

3. Rest for a few moments, and then run at moderate speed for 50 meters with straight, hard legs and a cadence of 180 steps per minute, landing on a heel with each step.

4. Rest briefly, and then run for 50 meters at a moderate speed with a cadence of 180 steps per minute and with soft, slightly flexed knees at ground contact, making sure that each landing occurs on the midfoot region.

5. Repeat Steps 1 through 4 one more time.

At first, make sure that the contrast running is carried out on a soft, forgiving surface such as grass, beach sand, a gym floor, or a rubberized track. During each 50-meter segment, be aware of how different each running style feels and how the midfoot-striking leads to springier, more comfortable running with less perceived effort and discomfort. Contrast running helps to reinforce the form essentials of midfoot-landings, "springy" legs, and good cadence.

Summary

Compared with heel-striking, midfoot-striking reduces the rate at which impact forces travel up the leg and therefore decreases the risk of injury. However, a shift from heel- to midfoot- striking can actually increase the chance of injury, if it is not carried out in a careful and gradual manner. Five phases of drills, plus contrast running, can gradually transform a runner's ground-contact pattern from heel- to midfoot-striking over time. When the drills are performed with a gradual change in training (so that a runner is spending progressively less training time in heel-striking mode), eventually "drilling" and running will merge, and a runner will become a full-fledged midfoot-striker with faster running performances and less risk of injury.

References

1. C. McDougall, *Born to Run* (Knopf, New York: Vintage, 2009).

7

Upgrading Shank Angle

It takes just a few seconds to make the change from heel- to midfoot-striking during drills. The transformation from a large shank angle at touchdown (SAT) to the optimal six- to seven-degree angle is similarly brief. However, the total change—to where all running is completed with an SAT of six to seven degrees—can take several months, similar to the time frame sometimes associated with the change from heel- to midfoot-striking (figure 7.1).

As mentioned in chapter 6, the reason for the long conversion period is not because it takes a long time to learn how to react with the ground in a different way. Most runners with a large SAT can reduce those lofty angles nearly instantly during drills. However, they often will not preserve the more minimal SAT when they change from carrying out the initial shank-angle-minimizing drills to regular running. Many will broaden SAT again as they move from drills to running, because a broad SAT is what their neuromuscular systems are accustomed to producing. The human neuro-muscular system is not usually agreeable to sudden, complete changes in running kinematics, even when the capacity to make such alterations is present.

We shouldn't be angry at our neuromuscular systems for this. After all, just as was the case with the change from heel- to midfoot-striking, a severe reduction in SAT changes everything. When shank angle changes, the leg muscles and connective tissues begin working in completely differ-ent ways, and muscles that had been relatively inactive during big-shank-angle running (especially the calf muscles) suddenly begin carrying out a

Figure 7.1 It can take months for a runner to transform completely from (*a*) a high SAT to (*b*) a six- or seven-degree SAT.

heavy load of work with each step. While it is highly beneficial to make the change from big SAT to six- or seven-degree landings, an acute change can actually hurt running economy and increase the risk of injury in the short term. Going for an 8-mile run with a small SAT after years of running with a big SAT is a recipe for serious calf discomfort.

The Danger of Sudden Changes in SAT

Why is a sudden change in SAT such a bad idea, even though long-term reduction in shank angle is a fantastic concept? Hitting the ground with a more flexed knee, and moving the foot back so that it strikes closer to a point under a runner's center of mass, tends to change not just the shank angle, but also the way in which the foot hits the ground. Specifically, moving the foot closer to the body so that shank angle is smaller tends to push a runner toward midfoot- striking rather than heel-striking (figures 7.2 and 7.3).

If you doubt that this is the case, try a simple drill: Stand with fairly erect posture, with your feet directly under your shoulders and your knees "soft" (relaxed) and a little flexed, and then begin running in place. Do you notice how the mid-regions of your feet (or even the balls of your feet) are hitting the ground? Now try running in place with the same posture using a heel-striking pattern. Do you notice how uncomfortable this is? Moving the feet back so that each impact with the ground occurs closer to a point under the center of the body tends to naturally produce a midfoot-landing pattern (figure 7.4a and b).

Figure 7.2 **When a runner lands on her heel with a relatively straight leg, her SAT is usually quite fat.**

Figure 7.3 **Making initial contact with the ground with a less-straight leg (more flexion at the knee) and smaller SAT automatically pushes a runner away from heel-striking and toward midfoot landings.**

Figure 7.4 Reducing shank angle at initial impact tends to naturally enforce a shift from (*a*) heel-striking to (*b*) midfoot-striking. Heel-striking becomes too uncomfortable for the pattern to persist.

All of this being true, we are left with a scenario similar to the one observed during the change from heel-striking to midfoot-striking. The greater reliance on smaller shank angles (and the associated move toward midfoot-striking) reduces the vertical loading rate of force through the shank and entire rest of the leg. Use of more abbreviated shank angles is gentle on the knees and hips. This prevents the unmitigated effects of Isaac Newton's equal-and-opposite reactions from blasting the knees and hips with tremendous forces directly up the legs from the heels on each step. Smaller shank angles are comforting to the muscles and connective tissues of the shins, too, because they reduce the eccentric control of slap-down work that the muscles, tendons, and ligaments must carry out when SAT is large and heel-striking is dominant (figure 7.5).

Figure 7.5 After a heel strike, when the foot hits the ground, the shin muscles are working hard to control the foot while simultaneously being stretched. This eccentric action increases the risk of stress reactions in the tibia and fibula as well as damage to the muscles and tendons of the shin.

Drawbacks of Landing With Lower SATs

It is important to note that moving the foot back toward the body and reducing the SAT converts the calf muscles and Achilles tendon from lazy passengers during gait to the hardest-working members of the below-the-knee team. This has to be true because the ankle making a small shank angle begins to undergo dorsiflexion immediately after impact, with the top of the foot moving closer to the shin instead of away from it (as it does during the slap-down of the foot associated with a big SAT). As mentioned in chapter 6, this dorsiflexion after touchdown places extra strain on the Achilles tendon and calf-muscle complex (gastrocnemius and soleus), which must work together to control the strong dorsiflexion approximately 90 times per minute per ankle (assuming a decent cadence of 180 steps per minute) (figures 7.6 and 7.7).

Over the long term, of course, it's good to ask the Achilles tendon and calf muscles to carry out more work per step because this additional work can gradually strengthen those key areas of the lower limbs. However, sudden jumps in work output, especially when performed 90 times per minute per

Figure 7.6   With heel-striking and a large SAT, the initial ankle action after contact with the ground will be plantar flexion, with large forces placed on the shin muscles and tendons to control this plantar flexion.

Figure 7.7   With a small shank angle (and a foot strike that is usually closer to midfoot), the initial ankle action tends to be dorsiflexion, with large forces placed on the controlling Achilles tendon and calf muscles.

foot, can have a crippling effect on the Achilles tendon and calf muscles, producing soreness and tightness that can persist for days (or a significant calf injury which can last even longer).

The problem associated with such an injury is not with low SAT (or even with the increased reliance on midfoot-striking), but rather with an overly dramatic and sudden transition from big to little SATs. As outlined in chapter 6, transformations of form and training always require a slow and careful approach in order to minimize the risk of injury. Runners working toward smaller SATs should make a very gradual entry into this new form pattern, instead of an all-or-nothing approach over a short period of time.

A gradual transition from large to six- to seven-degree SAT is especially important for the high-volume runner. Runners who have a big SAT and are averaging five miles of running per week can probably immediately begin hitting 20 percent of their miles (about one mile per week) with low shank angles and no negative consequences. The runner who averages 70 miles per week, on the other hand, would be in trouble at 20 percent (14 miles per week) at low shank angle, especially if most of the miles were covered in a single run. The calves, Achilles tendons, and metatarsal bones of the feet would be at heightened risk of injury.

The change from expanded to diminutive shank angles will produce significant benefits (table 7.1). As previously described, impact-force-loading rate in the leg (VALR) will decrease. The knees and hips will get a much-needed break, and braking forces during stance will be reduced. The time spent producing braking forces (as opposed to propulsive forces) during stance will shorten, and thus a greater fraction of stance will be devoted to pushing the runner forward. Economy will improve, in part because of the reduced braking forces, as less energy and oxygen will be needed to overcome braking. Economy will also improve because of the shorter duration of the braking phase. This will reduce stance time and thus the amount of oxygen utilized with each step to support the body. Propulsive forces will increase because the legs will become springier. Increased propulsive forces will lead to a higher performance potential. Risk of injury will be lower because of the lower force-loading rate.

TABLE 7.1

FACTORS ASSOCIATED WITH HIGH VS LOW SAT

	High SAT	6–7 degree SAT
Force loading rate	High	Reduced
Breaking forces during stance	High	Reduced
Time spent producing breaking forces	Long	Short
Running economy	Poor	Improved
Oxygen Required to overcome breaking	High	Reduced
Stance time	Longer	Shorter
Stride rate	Slower	Faster
Risk of injury	Higher	Lower

Running With Battering Rams or Springs

A key point to remember is that the runner with a big shank angle usually hits the ground with a relatively straight leg, with the landing foot well in front of the body. In contrast, the runner with a small shank angle hits the ground with the foot closer to the body (and the body's center of mass), and with a "softer" and more flexed knee compared with heel-striking. Small SATs provide milder landings, with impact force travelling up the leg at a lower speed. Running fast with high shank angles forces the runner to ram a leg into the ground at high speed with each step, while running quickly with low shank angles brings your feet back and allows your legs to work like the springier structures they were intended to be (figure 7.8).

If there remains any doubt that big shin angles put runners more at risk for injury than small shin angles, consider this scenario: You are running along a sidewalk at high speed and come to the end of the block. There, you must spring forward off of the curb and land on a cement roadway that is 2 feet, or .6 meters, below the top level of the curb. You are going to jump down onto the road at high velocity, and you must land on just one foot. Would you rather land on your heel, with your foot well out in front of you and with a straight, rigid leg? Or would you rather land midfoot, with your foot closer to being under your body and your knee flexed to absorb the impact shock? Which plan carries the greater risk of injury?

Figure 7.8 A small SAT allows the leg to function like a shock-absorbing spring, rather than a high-impact battering ram.

Drills for Shank Angle Transitioning

On the pages that follow, you will find drills to facilitate the transition from large to small SATs. They should be carried out barefoot at first in order to provide superior proprioception and therefore a better feeling for midfoot-striking and smaller shank angles (figure 7.9). Developing this feeling will help sustain midfoot-landings and small SATs during training and races. All drill durations are measured in minutes.

Figure 7.9 Jogging barefoot helps runners learn to land midfoot with low SATs.

PHASE ONE: BAREFOOT

Activity	Duration (minutes)	Stance
Walk in place with midfoot landing and small shank angle at initial impact	1:00	Soft, flexed knees
Jog in place with midfoot-landing and small SAT	3:00	Soft, flexed knees
Jog forward with midfoot-landing and small SAT	3:00	Soft, flexed knees and small steps

Conduct the drills before the main portion of your overall workout. Repeat the drills about five times per week for two weeks, or until you are completely certain that you can carry out all three activities with midfoot-landings and small SATs. Verify this by video analysis using a smart phone or camera capable of recording at 240 fps or greater along with an analysis app. You are then ready to move on to Phase Two.

PHASE TWO: IN RUNNING SHOES

Activity	Duration (minutes)	Stance
Walking in place with midfoot-landing and small SAT	1:00	Soft, flexed knees
Jog in place with midfoot-landing and small SAT	3:00	Soft, flexed knees
Jog forward with midfoot-landing and small SAT	3:00	Soft, flexed knees and small steps

Complete the drills about five times per week for two weeks, or until you are completely certain that you can carry out all three activities with midfoot-landings and low shank angles while shod. Verify this by video analysis using a smart phone or camera capable of recording at 240 fps or greater, along with an analysis app. You are then ready to move on to Phase Three.

PHASE THREE: BAREFOOT

Activity	Duration (minutes)	Stance
Jog in place with midfoot-landing and small SAT	1:00	Soft, flexed knees
Jog forward with midfoot-landing and small SAT	3:00	Soft, flexed knees and small steps
Run forward with midfoot-landing and small SAT	3:00	Soft, flexed knees and longer steps

When running forward, move at medium to medium-hard intensity, somewhat like a half-marathon to 10K race pace. Warm up properly before you carry out Phase Three. Complete the drills about five times per week for two weeks, or until you are completely certain that you can carry out all three activities with midfoot-landings and small shank angles while barefoot. Verify by video analysis using a smart phone or camera capable of recording at 240 fps or greater, along with an analysis app. You are then ready to move on to Phase Four.

PHASE FOUR: IN RUNNING SHOES

Activity	Duration (minutes)	Stance
Jog in place with midfoot-landing and small SAT	1:00	Soft, flexed knees
Jog forward with midfoot-landing and small SAT	3:00	Soft, flexed knees and small steps
Run forward with midfoot-landing and small SAT	3:00	Soft, flexed knees and longer steps

When running forward, move at medium to medium-hard intensity (somewhat like half-marathon to 10K race pace, or a little faster). Warm up properly before you carry out Phase Four. Complete the drills about five times per week for two weeks, or until you are completely certain that you can carry out all three activities with midfoot-landings and small SATs while shod in your regular training or racing shoes. Verify by video analysis using a smart phone or camera capable of recording at 240 fps or greater, along with an analysis app. You are then ready to move on to more complicated drills described in subsequent chapters.

These drills take seven minutes per workout to complete. For the rest of your training session (including during the warm-up), gradually introduce more and more running with midfoot-landings and low SATs. For example, during the first week of drills, you may want to focus on running with midfoot-striking and low SATs for about 10 percent of your normal training time; the rest of the time, simply run normally. During the second week of drills, transition to running with midfoot-striking and small SATs for around 20 percent of your training time, and so on.

Contrast Runs

A couple of times per week, after an adequate warm-up, supplement the above drills with contrast runs, proceeding as follows:

1. Run at moderate speed for approximately 50 meters with straight, stiff legs, with little knee flexion and the landing point well ahead of the body (large SAT).
2. Rest for a few moments, and then run 50 meters at moderate speed with soft, slightly flexed knees.
3. Rest for a few moments, and then run 50 meters with straight, hard legs, landing on a heel with each step and with large SAT.
4. Rest briefly, and then run 50 meters at moderate speed with soft, slightly flexed knees, making sure that each landing occurs at the midfoot with small SAT.
5. Repeat Steps 1 through 4 two more times.

At first, make sure that the contrast running is carried out on a soft, forgiving surface such as grass, sand, a gym floor, or a rubberized track. During each 50-meter segment, be aware of how different each running style feels—and how midfoot-striking with small shank angles leads to springier running with less discomfort and lower perceived effort.

Summary

The transition from large SAT to a six- or seven-degree SAT will occur at different rates for individual runners; some runners may make the transformation nearly instantly while others might require several months. Regular performance of the drills described in this chapter will facilitate the transition. But remember that runners should not try to transition all running from large SAT to small SAT in a short period of time. The change should be made progressively to prevent injury to the Achilles tendon, calf muscles, and feet. As drills are completed week by week, an individual's running will gradually and progressively become more like the drills. Then, the transformation from large to small SATs will be complete.

8

Shortening Stance Time and Increasing Cadence

To become a faster runner, it's important to increase cadence (steps per minute) by shortening stance time (amount of time spent on the ground per step). After all, speed is defined by the equation Step Rate × Step Length = Running Velocity.

Running speed (velocity) is expressed in meters per second, step rate in steps per second, and step length as meters travelled per step.

To understand how a shortened stance time can help increase cadence and upgrade speed, consider the case of a 5K competitor who is currently running her 5Ks in about 18 minutes flat and wants to improve. Her average velocity during her current 5Ks can be expressed by the equation 5,000 meters ÷ 18 minutes (1,080 seconds) = 4.63 meters per second.

Now, this speed of 4.63 meters per second is a function of step rate and step length, as expressed in the above equation for running velocity. For illustration purposes, let's say that our runner is a "typical" competitor, meaning she would take about 164 steps per minute during a 5K. This allows us to fill out the rest of the information in the 5K equation: 164 steps per minute is a cadence of 164/60 = 2.73 steps per second. Plugging this value into the 5K equation reveals:

4.63 meters per second = 2.73 steps per second × step length

And thus:

4.63 meters per second ÷ 2.73 steps per second = 1.7 meters per step (step length)

So now we know exactly what she is doing during her 5Ks, and we know that she can increase her 5K speed by either (a) expanding step length without harming step rate, or (b) upgrading step rate without reducing step length. Either way, she will have a faster speed during her 5Ks. Of course, she could do both simultaneously, but let's keep things simple for now.

Expand Step Length or Increase Step Rate?

Working on expanding step length is probably not a good idea for now. For one thing, we have indicated in this scenario that the runner is "typical" and is therefore probably running with an abnormally and unproductively large shank angle at initial impact with the ground (SAT). If we tell her to increase her step length, she will probably reach out even farther with each step, increasing her SAT and thus also magnifying her braking forces at impact and fattening her stance-phase duration of gait. This of course would hurt step rate and be counterproductive. We can also mention here that it would hurt her running economy (the oxygen cost of running).

But increasing her step rate (and thus cadence) produces an entirely different scenario. It is true that to achieve a higher cadence she will initially take shorter steps; this will produce less "air time" for her leg and foot so she can contact the ground more quickly, which leads to a natural increase in step rate. However, as she becomes accustomed to the higher cadence, her step length will organically and spontaneously return to the previous dimension, especially if she incorporates the movements and drills described in the rest of this chapter. This return can produce a notable upswing in 5K performance because she will be taking more steps per second while preserving her step length.

Let's say that our runner increases her cadence from the sub-optimal 164 steps per minute (which she has been locked into for years) to an optimal 180 steps per minute (three steps per second) without thwarting step length. Returning to a familiar equation, she is now ready to run her 5Ks in the following way:

$$5\text{K Speed} = \text{Step Rate} \times \text{Step Length}$$

$$5\text{K speed (new)} = 3 \text{ steps per second} \times 1.7 \text{ meters per step} = 5.1 \text{ meters per second}$$

This certainly seems a lot better than her previous 5K speed of 4.63 meters per second. It will produce an improvement in finishing time from the prior 18:00 to a new personal record: 5,000/5.1 = 980 seconds, or 16:20! The 9.8 percent increase in step rate (without a sacrifice in step length) produced a similarly large gain in 5K running speed and a 100-second upgrade in overall 5K performance.

Tweaking Cadence to Become a Faster Runner

Of course, it is important to advance step rate without harming step length. This is accomplished in two ways: First, by incorporating drills that—somewhat paradoxically—temporarily reduce step length so that runners can literally use "baby steps" to develop a neuromuscular mastery of higher cadence. Such drills are described later in this chapter.

Second, a runner should try to upgrade the capacity to produce the usual amount of propulsive force but during a shorter period of time when the foot is on the ground (during stance). Since the same propulsive force is produced, step length is not harmed. However, as that force is produced in a shorter period of time, step rate advances, and the runner will be faster than before.

It would be even better to produce more propulsive force than usual and to produce it with a shorter stance time, as this would create an even-greater upswing in running velocity. The explosive activities outlined at the end of this chapter make it possible for a runner to produce the usual (or greater) propulsive force with a shorter stance time.

Drills for Transitioning to a Higher Cadence

On the pages that follow, you will find drills to facilitate the transition to a higher cadence. They should be carried out barefoot at first in order to provide superior proprioception and therefore a better feeling for ground-reaction time. Developing this feeling will help sustain a higher cadence during both training and races. All drill durations are measured in minutes. Use a loud, beeping metronome to keep cadence at 180 steps per minute for each drill and keep soft, flexed knees for each set.

PHASE ONE: BAREFOOT

Activity	Duration (minutes)
Walk in place with midfoot-landing and small SAT	1:00
Jog in place with midfoot-landing and small SAT	3:00
Jog forward with midfoot-landing, small SAT, and small steps	3:00

Conduct the drills before the main portion of your overall workout. Complete the drills about five times per week for two weeks, or until you are completely certain that you can carry out all three activities with midfoot-landings, small SATs, and a cadence of 180. Verify with video analysis using a smartphone or camera capable of recording at 240 fps or greater, along with an analysis app. You are then ready to move on to Phase Two.

PHASE TWO: IN RUNNING SHOES

Activity	Duration (minutes)
Walk in place with midfoot-landing and small SAT	1:00
Jog in place with midfoot-landing and small SAT	3:00
Jog forward with midfoot-landing, small SAT, and small steps	3:00

Complete the drills about five times per week for two weeks, or until you are completely certain that you can carry out all three activities with midfoot-landings, small SATs, and a cadence of 180 steps per minute while shod. Verify with video analysis using a smart phone or camera capable of recording at 240 fps or greater, along with an analysis app. You are then ready to move on to Phase Three.

PHASE THREE: BAREFOOT

Activity	Duration (minutes)
Jog in place with midfoot-landing and small SAT	1:00
Jog forward with midfoot-landing and small SAT	3:00
Run forward with midfoot-landing and small SAT	3:00

Running forward means moving along at medium to medium-hard intensity (somewhat like a half-marathon to 10K race pace). Complete the drills about five times per week for two weeks, or until you are completely certain that you can carry out all three activities with midfoot-landings, small shank angles, and a cadence of 180 while barefoot. Verify with video analysis using a smart phone or camera capable of recording at 240 fps or greater, along with an analysis app. You are then ready to move on to Phase Four.

PHASE FOUR: IN RUNNING SHOES

Activity	Duration (minutes)
Jog in place with midfoot-landing and SAT	1:00
Jog forward with midfoot-landing and small SAT	3:00
Run forward with midfoot-landing, small SAT, and small steps	3:00

Running forward means moving along at medium to medium-hard intensity (like half-marathon to 10 K race pace or a little faster). Complete the drills about five times per week for two weeks, or until you are completely certain that you can carry out all three activities with midfoot-landings, small shank angles, and a 180 cadence while shod in your regular training or racing shoes. Verify with video analysis using a smart-phone or camera capable of recording at 240 fps or greater, along with an analysis app.

Please note: All drills take seven minutes to complete. For the rest of your training session, including any additional warm-up activities, gradually introduce more and more running with midfoot-landings, low SATs, and high cadence. For example, during the first week of Phase One, you may want to focus on running with midfoot-strikes, low SATs, and a 180 cadence for about 10 percent of your normal training time; the rest of the time, simply run normally. During the second week of drills, move up to running with midfoot-striking, small shank angles, and a 180 cadence for around 20 percent of your training time, and so on. This will help to prevent acute stress on the metatarsals of your feet and your calf muscles as you make your form transition.

Contrast Runs

A couple of times per week, after an adequate warm-up, supplement the drills (Phase One through Phase Four) with contrast runs. At first, make sure that the contrast running is carried out on a soft, forgiving surface such as grass, sand, a gym floor, or a rubberized track. During each one-minute segment, be aware of how different each type of running feels—and how midfoot-striking with small SATs and high cadence leads to springier, more comfortable running with lower perceived effort.

Cadence Contrast Runs

1. Run barefoot at moderate speed for one minute with midfoot-landings, SAT of about six degrees, and a cadence of 180 steps per minute as coordinated by a metronome.

2. Rest for a few moments, and then run barefooted for one minute at moderate speed with midfoot-landings, SAT of six degrees, and a cadence of 200 steps per minute.

3. Rest for a few moments, and then repeat Step 1.

4. Put on training or racing shoes, and then conduct Steps 1 through 3 one more time.

Contrast running helps runners truly experience and feel the difference between various cadences and can strongly reinforce the habits of landing midfooted with low SATs and a high cadence. Practicing with a cadence of 200 and then decreasing to 180 steps per minute is particularly effective at establishing 180 as the *de facto* cadence.

Landing Contrast Runs

1. While barefoot, on an extremely pliant surface like soft grass, run for 20 seconds with a cadence of 180 and the deliberate use of heel-strikes as the preferred landing pattern.

2. Rest for a moment, and then (again while barefoot and on the same pliant surface) run for 40 seconds with a cadence of 180 and the deliberate use of midfoot-strikes as the preferred landing pattern.

3. On any surface, repeat Steps 1 and 2, this time while shod in your normal training or racing shoes.

Contrast running helps runners truly experience and feel the difference between heel-striking and midfoot-landing and can strongly reinforce the habits of landing midfooted with low SATs. Practicing with a heel-strike pattern and then changing over to midfoot-striking is particularly effective for experiencing the inherent awkwardness of heel-striking and the higher rate of loading of impact forces associated with hitting the ground with the heels.

Explosive Workout Routines

Explosive routines are designed to decrease stance time and increase cadence while simultaneously advancing step length. When carrying out the explosive drills, please make sure that all of these cadence-enhancing activities are completed on a forgiving surface such as soft dirt, grass, cushioned artificial turf, a compliant track, or a wooden gym floor. Complete the explosive routines approximately twice per week during the phase of training in which you are directly working on advancing running speed. During other phases of training, use these drills less often—although you may want to use subsets of the drills as part of your warm-up routine. However, do not use these explosive activities until you have established a good base of running-specific strength (see chapter 14).

Explosive Drills

1. WARM UP

Start with about 12 minutes of light running, taking a few moments to lightly stretch any tight areas. Complete a couple of short (approximately 60-meter) "stride-outs" at about 5 K race speed.

2. SKIPPING

1. Skip on the balls of your feet for 30 seconds, using very quick leg action (figure 8.1).
2. Keep your feet on the ground for a minimal amount of time as you skip.
3. Rest for a moment, and then repeat.

Figure 8.1   **Explosive skipping helps runners develop the capacity to minimize stance time.**

3. DOUBLE-LEG HURDLE JUMPS

1. Position eight hurdles in a neat row, 45 inches (about 1 meter) apart, with the height of each hurdle set at 24 inches (.6 meters).

2. Starting from one end, jump over each hurdle, taking off and landing on two legs until all eight hurdles have been cleared in continuous movement (figure 8.2). Be as explosive as possible, minimizing ground-contact time with each landing.

3. Once you have cleared the last hurdle, jog back to the start and repeat the whole cycle three more times.

Avoid taking an extra hop between hurdles. There should be just one ground contact between the barriers. As explosive strength improves, the number of reps can increase, and the jumps can change to hops, with the activity carried out on one leg at a time.

Figure 8.2 Hopping over hurdles can help runners develop explosive reactions with high propulsive force and thus lead to higher stepping rates and longer steps while running.

4. ONE-LEG HOPS IN PLACE

1. Stand with your left foot forward and your right foot back, with the feet about one shin-length apart. From side to side, the feet should be hip-width apart.

2. Place the toes of your right foot on a block or step that is six to eight inches (15 to 20 centimeters) high. All of your weight should be directed through the middle-to-ball portion of your left foot.

3. Hop rapidly on your left foot at a cadence of 2.5 to 3 hops per second (25 to 30 foot contacts per 10 seconds) for 40 seconds (figure 8.3). As you do so, your left knee should rise by about four to six inches (10 to 15 centimeters) with each upward hop, while your right leg and foot should remain stationary. Your left foot should strike the ground midfooted and spring upward rapidly, as though it were contacting a very hot stove burner. The hips should remain fairly level and virtually motionless throughout the exercise, with very little vertical displacement.

4. After completing the first set, rest for a moment and then repeat the one-leg-hopping action on your right leg, also for 40 seconds. Rest again, and perform one more set on each leg.

Figure 8.3 **Hopping on one leg in place can help runners develop the capacity to react quickly with the ground and shorten stance times.**

5. DIAGONAL HOP

1. To diagonal-hop, for a prescribed time period of 45 seconds, start by jogging for a few strides and then move diagonally to the right with your right foot (figure 8.4a).

2. When your right foot makes contact with the ground, quickly hop once in place.

3. When your right foot comes down to earth after this single hop, explosively hop diagonally to the left, landing on your left foot (figure 8.4b).

4. When your left foot hits the ground, hop once in place and then explode diagonally to the right. Your right foot will then strike the ground, and you will hop once and then "explode" diagonally to the left, and so on.

5. Stay relaxed at all times as you carry out this drill. Try to move in a rhythmic and coordinated manner. Look ahead, not at your feet.

6. Rest for 15 seconds, and then hop diagonally for 45 more seconds.

Figure 8.4 **Hopping diagonally promotes explosive contacts with the ground and the shortening of stance times, while enhancing ankle strength and reactivity.**

6. ONE-LEG SQUATS WITH JUMPS

1. These are just like regular one-leg squats (figure 8.5a), except that you will jump high in the air when ascending after each squat (figure 8.5b).
2. When returning to earth after each vertical jump, land smoothly and then immediately and with good coordination begin the next squat.
3. Complete two sets of 10 reps per leg.

Figure 8.5   One-leg squats with jumps convert traditional one-leg squats into dynamic activities. These squats improve a runner's ability to produce force quickly during ground contact and shorten stance time.

7. GREYHOUND RUNS

Carry these out in an area that has at least 100 meters of unobstructed surface.

1. Accelerate for 20 meters and hold close-to-max pace for 80 meters (figure 8.6).

2. Rest for 20 to 30 seconds after the 100-meter burst by walking around, and then repeat your high-speed running in the opposite direction.

3. You are finished with this drill when you have completed eight 100-meter sprints (four in each direction). Be especially careful to avoid "over-striding," or reaching out with each foot and landing with large SAT.

Figure 8.6 Greyhound runs can improve a runner's capacity to react with the ground explosively and use higher stride rates to advance speed.

8. ONE-LEG SQUATS WITH LATERAL HOPS

1. To carry out the one-leg squats with lateral hops, stand with your left foot forward and your right foot back, with your feet about one shin-length apart. From side to side, the feet should be hip-width apart.

2. If possible, place the toes of your right foot on a block or step that is six to eight inches (15 to 20 centimeters) high. Most of your weight should be directed through the mid-sole of your left foot.

3. Bend your left leg and lower your body until your left knee creates a 90-degree angle between the thigh and lower leg (figure 8.7a).

4. Once your left knee reaches an angle of 90 degrees, hop laterally with your left foot about six to 10 inches (15 to 25 centimeters). Be sure your right foot stays in place (figure 8.7b).

5. Hop back to the center position, and then hop medially (to the right when your left leg is forward) for six to 10 inches (15 to 25 centimeters), before coming back to the center position.

6. Return to the starting (straight leg) position, while maintaining an upright trunk posture. That completes one rep.

7. Perform 2×12 sets on each leg, with a one-minute break between sets.

When you hop laterally and medially, be sure to keep the toes of your hopping foot pointed straight ahead. Also, be certain to perform a squat which narrows the angle between the back of your thigh and the back of your shank to close to 90 degrees in each position (medial and lateral, as well as center).

Figure 8.7 One-leg squats with lateral hops can improve a runner's ability to react quickly with the ground and shorten stance time, while simultaneously improving leg stability and strength.

9. HIGH-KNEE EXPLOSIONS

1. To carry these out, stand with straight but relaxed posture, with your feet directly below your shoulders.

2. Begin by jumping very lightly in place. Then suddenly—while remaining in that straight posture—jump vertically while swinging both knees up toward your chest (figure 8.8).

3. Land on your feet in a relaxed and resilient manner, and then repeat step 2 14 more times.

4. Once you've completed the 15 repetitions, rest for a few seconds, and then conduct 15 more reps.

Do not carry out the explosive action by hunching your upper body forward to meet your knees; your upper body should be fairly erect at all times. The key action is the dramatic upward acceleration of the knees toward the chest. As you become skilled with this exercise, progress to conducting the high-knee explosions on one leg at a time.

Figure 8.8 **High-knee explosions improve reactivity with the ground and thus shorten stance time while advancing the overall power of the legs.**

10. SHANE'S IN-PLACE ACCELERATIONS (SIPAs)

1. To carry these out, stand with straight but relaxed posture, with your feet directly below your shoulders.

2. Begin by simply jogging in place, but then—when you feel ready—begin to dramatically increase your in-place stepping rate, building up fairly quickly to as rapid a cadence as you can sustain (figure 8.9). Remember that you are not moving forward significantly as you complete this drill.

3. Maintain a straight but relaxed posture, and keep your feet close to the ground as you do this. You are not shooting for high knee lift, but rather for minimal foot-contact times.

4. Perform three sets of 20 seconds each.

When you are learning this exercise, it sometimes helps to turn your legs slightly outward at the hips as you build up toward top speed. Lean forward slightly from the ankles as you run explosively in place.

Figure 8.9 **Shane's In-Place Accelerations can enhance the ability to run with a higher stepping rate. Lean forward slightly from the ankles as you run explosively in place.**

11. DOWNHILL HOPS

1. Hop 3×20 meters on each leg, quickly and with good coordination, on a hill that provides a 3- to 5-percent decline (figure 8.10).

2. Hop back up the 20-meter slope after each descent.

3. Rest very briefly at the bottom after each hop down and again at the top after each hop up.

Figure 8.10 Hopping downhill helps runners coordinate foot-strikes when their feet are moving at higher velocities (from the downward acceleration associated with each downhill hop). This improves coordination at high running speeds and shortens stance times.

12. DOWNHILL RUNNING

1. Run very fast downhill for 70 to 100 meters, using a midfoot-strike pattern (figure 8.11).
2. Jog easily back up after each run-down to recover.
3. Complete four of these very quick descents.

Figure 8.11   Like hopping downhill, running downhill helps runners coordinate their foot-strikes more effectively when their feet and legs are moving at higher velocities. Ultimately, this can shorten stance times and augment cadence and power

13. 4 × 400

1. While staying relaxed and running rhythmically, run the 400s at a pace that is faster than your best one-mile pace, using high cadence and great overall form (figure 8.12).
2. Employ two-minute jog recoveries in between the 400s.

Figure 8.12 **Running 400s at high velocity with a strong cadence, midfoot-landings, and low SAT helps to improve maximal running speed.**

14. COOL DOWN

Complete about two miles, or 3.2 kilometers, of light running.

Summary

Shortening stance time and increasing running cadence are essential and fundamental upgrades in form which improve maximal running velocity and overall running performance. A metronome set at 180 and above, employed with drills which emphasize small SATs and midfoot landings, can be used to help advance cadence. Contrast running is another effective way to heighten the rate at which the feet hit the ground. Explosive training that incorporates a variety of drills can simultaneously shorten stance time and augment cadence, while upgrading propulsive power. The results of these important activities will include faster running speeds during training and much-improved race performances.

9

Improving Body Lean

Chapters 4 and 7 explored how shank angle at touchdown (SAT) is critically important. If the shank angle is large and positive, a massive braking force is produced, which slows running speed. Large shank angle also tends to dictate heel-striking over midfoot- and forefoot-strikes, thus spiking loading rates of impact forces on the leg and increasing the risk of injury.

In contrast, a negative SAT reduces the magnitude of both vertical and horizontal propulsive forces and thus limits running speed. A shank angle that is barely positive (approximately six degrees) is linked with the best-possible running, from the standpoints of both performance and injury prevention. A six-degree SAT allows the leg to absorb and store impact forces during the first moments of stance, and then places the leg in optimal position to create the best possible vertical and horizontal propulsive forces (optimizing running velocity and economy).

Compared with shank angle, the effects of body lean on performance and injury risk are not as strong but are nonetheless important. Body lean can be defined as the position of the body relative to vertical at three key stages of stance:

1. At initial impact with the ground
2. At mid-stance
3. At toe-off

There is little scientific research available to guide us toward the establishment of optimal lean, so logic and experience must prevail. Consider the effects of the three lean patterns on propulsive force during stance.

How Body Lean Impacts Running Velocity

Body lean at mid-stance—roughly halfway through the stance phase of gait, when the body is positioned more or less directly over the foot, the ankle is dorsiflexed, the knee is flexed, and the hip is also slightly flexed—is the time when maximal vertical propulsive forces can be created. This is partially because it is the natural, elastic extension of the ankle, knee, and hip that creates the propulsive forces required for forward movement.

To better understand the relationship between body lean and propulsive forces, imagine yourself lifting a large weight overhead. Would you have the greatest mechanical advantage and the largest lifting power if your body were leaning forward as you attempted the lift? Would it be best to lean backward as you moved the heavy mass? Obviously, you would have the greatest mechanical advantage and stability with your body in a vertical position (not leaning at all), and you could elevate the most weight with your body in a vertical placement.

However, this changes during running. Instead of lifting a weight overhead, a runner reacts with the ground to produce both vertical and horizontal propulsive forces. Picture three mid-stance scenarios:

a. Applying force to the ground with the whole body leaning backward
b. Applying force to the ground with the body straight up (no lean backward or forward)
c. Applying force to the ground with the whole body leaning forward slightly

In each of these cases, think of the body as positioned in a straight line from the feet to the head, with no bending at the hips.

In situation A, with the body leaning backward, the vertical forces applied to the ground tend to push the body upward and backward (figure 9.1). This is clearly sub-optimal. For optimal running performance, the body should be pushed up and ahead, not up and back. Any backward movement of the body will dampen running velocity.

Figure 9.1 When the body leans backward, vertical propulsive forces push the body up and backward.

Straight is the Most Popular Body Angle, but . . .

In situation B, vertical propulsive forces push the body neither forward nor backward, but rather straight up (figure 9.2).

Figure 9.2 When the body is straight up during stance, vertical propulsive forces push the body up—instead of up and forward.

Although much maligned in the popular running press, vertical propulsive forces are critically important in running. During high-speed running, for example, the vertical propulsive forces created during stance can be 10 times greater than the horizontal propulsive forces. Reduce these vertical propulsive forces, and running will slow considerably.

If this is difficult to understand, bear in mind that a runner's forward movement over the ground is always a result of the interplay between vertical and horizontal propulsive forces. Vertical forces push the body up, and horizontal forces push the body forward (figure 9.3). The resulting body movement in a forward direction over the ground can be expressed as a vector created by those two forces.

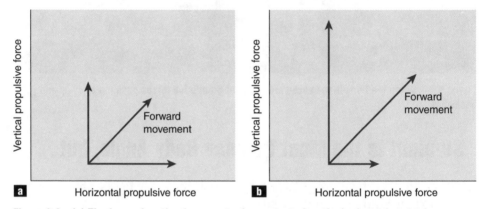

Figure 9.3 (*a*) The forward motion force vector is greatest when the horizontal vector is combined with a forward vertical vector. (*b*) Vertical propulsive forces are far more important than horizontal forces during high-speed running.

Thus, forward velocity is influenced by both vertical and horizontal forces, and—despite the widespread assumption in mainstream running media that vertical forces are bad—vertical forces have a greater impact on speed than horizontal forces. Usain Bolt creates the greatest vertical forces in the world during running. As mentioned, vertical forces can sometimes be 10 times greater than horizontal forces. This is counter-intuitive, given that the idea in running is to move forward, not upward, but it is nonetheless true.

Lean Determines Speed Vector

Body lean has a significant impact on the vector reflecting forward movement. If the body is leaning backward, that movement vector (the result of vertical and horizontal forces) will not be positioned as far forward.

If the body is straight up as propulsive forces are created, again the vector will not be as far forward. And if the body is inclined slightly forward, the vector will be directed farther forward—and thus will be more productive from the standpoint of forward movement, which is almost always a desired result during running (unless one is consciously trying to stop, in which case the body tends to naturally lean backward).

That said, a runner cannot incline the body too far forward in the hopes of producing the best forward vector (and thus running speed): Incline the body too far ahead, and there will be a profoundly negative effect on stride length. It will simply be too hard to get the leg and foot out ahead of the body when the body is tipped too far forward (figure 9.4).

Figure 9.4 **Excessive forward lean automatically decreases step length, a key element of speed.**

This means that a modest forward lean of the body (from the ankles, not the hips) is optimal. Experience with a wide array of runners, ranging in ability from the beginner to the super-elite, suggests that a lean of about five degrees is best (figure 9.5).

With a smaller lean, the body is too vertical as force is applied to the ground, which results in a movement vector that is pointed too far skyward. With a larger lean, the runner is on the verge of falling forward, and stride length is compromised.

Figure 9.5 A forward lean of approximately five degrees appears to be optimal.

Drills for Transitioning to a Better Body Lean

The following drills can facilitate the transition to a five-degree lean. They should be carried out barefoot at first, in order to provide superior proprioception and therefore a better feeling for body lean and position. All drill durations are measured in minutes. Maintain a cadence at 180 steps per minute for each drill and keep the knees soft and flexed for each set. Development of this feeling will help sustain the five-degree lean during both training and races (figure 9.6).

PHASE ONE: BAREFOOT

Activity	Duration (minutes)
Walk in place with midfoot-landing (while inclining the body forward about five degrees from the ankles)	1:00
Jog in place with midfoot-landing (while preserving a five-degree forward lean)	3:00
Jog forward with midfoot-landing, small SAT, and small steps using "baby steps" and a forward body lean of five degrees	3:00

Conduct Phase One before the main portion of your overall workout. Complete the drills as often as possible (at least two times per day). The goal is to be completely certain that you can carry out all the activities with four elements: midfoot-landings, small SATs, a cadence of 180, and a five-degree forward body lean. Verify this by video analysis using a smart phone or camera capable of recording at 240 fps or greater, along with an analysis app. Once you have achieved mastery of these four elements, you are ready to move on to Phase Two.

Figure 9.6 **Jogging in place, barefooted, with a forward lean of approximately five degrees can help to develop the capacity to run with an optimal forward lean.**

PHASE TWO: IN RUNNING SHOES

Activity	Duration (minutes)
Walk in place with midfoot-landing (plus forward body lean of five degrees, from the ankles)	1:00
Jog in place with midfoot-landing, and a forward body lean of five degrees	3:00
Jog forward with midfoot-landing, small SAT, and small "baby steps," while preserving a five-degree forward body lean	3:00

Complete Phase Two drills twice per day for two weeks, or until you have mastered optimal lean. Your goal is to be completely certain that you can carry out all three activities with midfoot-landings, small SATs, a cadence of 180 steps per minute while shod, and a forward body lean of five degrees. Verify this by video analysis using a smart phone or camera capable of recording at 240 fps or greater, along with an analysis app. Once mastery is attained, you are ready to move on to Phase Three.

PHASE THREE: BAREFOOT

Activity	Duration (minutes)
Jog in place with midfoot-landing and a forward body lean of five degrees	1:00
Jog forward with midfoot-landing, small SAT, and a forward body lean of five degrees	3:00
Run forward with midfoot-landing, small SAT, and a forward lean of five degrees	3:00

"Running forward" means moving along at medium to medium-hard intensity, somewhat like a half-marathon to 10K race pace. Complete Phase Three drills twice per day for two weeks or until you have mastered forward lean. The goal is to be completely certain that you can carry out all three activities with midfoot-landings, small SATs, high cadence (180 steps per minute), and five-degree lean while barefooted (figure 9.7). Verify by video analysis using a smartphone or a camera capable of recording at 240 fps or greater, along with an analysis app. You are then ready to move on to Phase Four.

Figure 9.7 **Running barefooted helps runners learn to land midfooted with low SAT and high cadence, plus proper forward body lean.**

PHASE FOUR: IN RUNNING SHOES

Activity	Duration (minutes)
Jog in place with midfoot-landing and a five-degree lean	1:00
Jog forward with midfoot-landing, small SAT, and a five-degree forward lean	3:00
Run forward with midfoot-landing, small SAT, small steps, and proper forward body lean	3:00

"Running forward" means moving along at medium to medium-hard intensity, somewhat like a half-marathon to 10K race pace, or a little faster. Complete Phase Four drills twice per day for two weeks, or until you are comfortable with optimal forward lean. The goal is to be completely certain that you can carry out all three activities with midfoot-landings, small SATs, a 180 cadence while shod in your regular training or racing shoes, and a forward body lean of five degrees. Verify by video analysis using a smart phone or a camera capable of recording at 240 fps or greater, along with an analysis app.

Please note that each of the four phases takes seven minutes to complete. If you are completing the lean drills prior to a workout, it is a good idea to gradually introduce more and more running with midfoot-landing, low SATs, high cadence, and a five-degree lean—for the rest of the training session, including the warm-up. For example, during your first week with the drills, it makes sense to focus on running with midfoot-strikes, low SATs, a cadence of 180 steps per minute, and a five-degree lean for about 10 percent of your normal workout duration. The rest of the time, simply run with your usual form. During the second week of drills, move up to running with midfoot-striking, small SATs, a cadence of 180 steps per minute, and a five-degree lean for around 20 percent of your training time, and so on.

Contrast Runs

A couple of times per week, after an adequate warm-up, supplement the above drills with contrast runs, as follows. At first, make sure that the contrast running is carried out on a soft, forgiving surface such as grass, sand, gym floor, or a rubberized track. During each one-minute segment, be aware of how different each lean pattern feels—and how the forward lean leads to springier, faster running with less discomfort and lower perceived effort.

1. Run barefoot at moderate speed for one minute with midfoot-landings, a six-degree SAT, a cadence of about 180 steps per minute, and a backward body lean (figure 9.8).

2. Rest for a few moments, and then run barefoot for one minute at moderate speed with midfoot-landings, a six-degree SAT, a cadence

of about 180 steps per minute, and the body held in a straight position (no lean).

3. Rest for a few moments, and then run barefoot for one minute at moderate speed with midfoot-landings, a six-degree SAT, a cadence of about 180 steps per minute, and the body held in the proper five-degree forward lean from the ankles.

4. Put on training or racing shoes, and then conduct Steps 1 through 3 one more time.

Figure 9.8 Contrast running helps runners truly experience and feel different body lean strategies and can strongly reinforce the habits of landing midfooted with low SATs, a high cadence, and good forward body lean.

Summary

When it comes to speed and performance, lean is not as important a factor as other key form characteristics (MSA, ROS, SAT, and FAT), but it nonetheless has an impact on running speed. As outlined in this chapter, an absence of lean and also backward lean change the vertical component of the propulsive-force vector, thus leading to reduced net propulsive forces and diminished running speeds. By contrast, forward lean pushes the propulsive-force vector in the desired direction: forward.

This should not be carried too far, however, as excessive forward lean may reduce step length and thus harm running velocity. A five-degree forward lean appears to be optimal.

Runners often vary their lean according to terrain, leaning forward more dramatically as they climb hills and leaning backward as they run downhill. These are natural reactions to terrain, but they should be consciously controlled. For example, excessive forward lean while climbing can lead to moving uphill with "baby steps," which slows velocity. Similarly, backward lean on downhills "applies the brakes" with each step and also leads to dramatically greater rates of impact-force loading on the legs. On the downhill, it is better to develop balance and coordination and preserve the slight forward lean (or at the very least, a vertical body position relative to the running surface). This will help to minimize braking and impact forces, and also "economize" running by letting gravity and elastic energy do most of the work.

Promoting Positive Posture

Posture in running is simply the alignment of—and the mechanical relationship between—the parts of the body that play a key role in the production of forward movement.

The Puzzle Pieces of Posture

The parts of the body that need to be positioned in a specific way to produce excellent running posture include:

- The feet and ankles
- The legs, including the knees
- The hips
- The trunk
- The arms, including the elbows and hands
- The head and neck

Each of these regions is associated with common postural flaws that can have a negative impact on running. Posture is adjusted not only for aesthetic reasons, but also to reduce the cost of running (running economy) and decrease fatigue in specific body regions. These actions bolster performance. Some postural adjustments—particularly those related to the feet, knees, and hips—should also decrease the risk of injury.

Common Posture Patterns

Runners tend to exhibit a variety of sub-optimal postural patterns, including the following areas.

Feet

The feet are often turned out during the stance phase of gait (figure 10.1). This actually shortens step length (a key component of speed) and may place undue strain on the insides of the ankles.

Knees

The knee is frequently extended when the foot collides with the ground, producing a relatively straight leg at impact with knees that are often stiffly locked. Straight legs and stiff knees amplify braking forces and reduce the ability of the knees to absorb and mitigate shock. This leads to the rapid transfer of impact force upward through the legs, hips, spine, neck, and head, thus increasing the risk of injury (figure 10.2). About 95 percent of runners run in this manner.

Figure 10.1 **Running with everted ankles can reduce both step length and speed.**

Figure 10.2 **Landing on the ground with stiff knees and straight legs increases the risk of injury.**

Hips

The hips are often either slouched with excessive posterior tilt or positioned with too much anterior tilt (figures 10.3a and b). Both of these postural setups can harm running, either by reducing net forward propulsive forces during stance or by directly limiting step length.

Figure 10.3　(*a*) Running with excessive posterior tilt of the pelvis can reduce step length. (*b*) Running with overly great anterior pelvic tilt can reduce forward propulsive forces.

Trunk

The trunk tends to rotate excessively (figure 10.4*a*) around the longitudinal axis of the body during forward movement. This creates activity like a washing machine, which eats up energy and harms running economy. The trunk is also often slouched slightly forward (kyphosis) (figure 10.4*b*) or pushed into a swayback position (lordosis) (figure 10.4*c*), which hurts propulsion and step length.

Figure 10.4 (*a*) Excessive rotational action of the trunk during running reflects a weak core and is likely linked with poor running economy. (*b*) A slouched-forward trunk reduces step length and can induce low-back strain and injury. (*c*) A pushed-back trunk can dampen running speed.

Arms

It is extremely common for the arms to create sub-optimal postural patterns in running. The arms may excessively cross the midline of the body during their forward swings. They may also be held too high or too far from the body, wasting oxygen and energy. Or the elbows may insufficiently drive backward during running—that is, the arms tend to remain in a forward position, with the elbows seldom venturing far behind the trunk. This creates excessive tightness in the shoulders and can potentially alter step rate. The arms should swing naturally during running, with the hand moving to the level of the hip during backswing and the elbow moving up to the hip during forward swing (figures 10.5a and b).

Figure 10.5   (*a*) The hand should be near the hip during backswing. (*b*) The elbow will be near the hip during forward swing of the arm.

Head and Neck

The most common problem with the head and neck is a forward tilt of the head during running, which wastes energy and creates tight, sore neck and upper back muscles (figure 10.6) The head should not lean forward, relative to the shoulders, but should be balanced in a vertical position above the trunk. Moving the head from side to side during gait is also an energy waster and should be avoided. In general, the shoulders should be relaxed and held back and down, not up and hunched forward.

Figure 10.6   A too-forward head during running can create tight, sore back muscles.

Posture Set-Up, Drills, and Cues

These common problems can be overcome, and correct posture can be achieved through the use of posture set-up drills and cues. Cues are simply mental reminders about proper body positions that lead to appropriate postural adjustments. Here are the cues a runner should use to set up optimal posture just before the beginning of any run, including a competitive effort:

Feet

The feet should be arranged so that they are aligned with each other, positioned directly under the shoulders, and pointed straight forward (figure 10.7).

Figure 10.7   Proper foot set-up prior to running.

Knees

The knees should be soft—slightly flexed, with just moderate tension in the quadricep muscles (figure 10.8*a*). Stiff, straight legs should be avoided (figure 10.8*b*).

Figure 10.8   (*a*) Proper knees before a run. (*b*) Excessively extended knees before running with consequentially straight legs.

Hips

Hips must not be tilted forward or backward, but should be centered (figure 10.9).

Figure 10.9   Centered hips prior to a run.

Posture

Overall posture is deliberately reset to avoid any whole-body flaws. To do this, align the feet, keep the knees soft, center the hips, and then reach the arms high overhead, stretching the entire body vertically as much as possible (figure 10.10).

Arms and Shoulders

Once the whole body is stretched out with the arms overhead, the arms and shoulders should relax, and the arms should be allowed to fall into place at the sides of the body. The combination of these two set-up steps (straightening the arms above the body and then letting them fall naturally) can be referred to with the verbal cue of "body tall, arms fall." This approach helps to eliminate problems associated with forward or backward inclinations of the hips or a slouching forward of the shoulders. After the "body tall, arms fall" procedure is carried out, the shoulders should be very relaxed and positioned slightly back, instead of slouched ahead of the trunk. Shoulders should be kept down instead of held high, thus conserving energy (figure 10.11).

Figure 10.10   **The whole body is stretched prior to beginning a run.**

Figure 10.11   Correct overall body posture after the "body-tall-arms-fall" movements.

Chin

The chin should be level, and eyes should be looking straight ahead, not at the ground. This helps prevent excessive flexion of the neck and the "forward-head" alignment, which can produce fatigue and tightness in the neck, shoulders, and upper back (figure 10.12).

Elbows

Elbows are bent "half-and-half." This means that the angle at the elbows is initially set to about 90 degrees. But then the arms are flexed even more at the elbow, in a relaxed way, so that the hands move about halfway toward the shoulders (figure 10.13).

Arms

Several alternating arm swings are completed from the position established after the hands are positioned halfway, with special attention paid to the avoidance of cross-swinging (bringing the hands across the body) and a specific focus on keeping arm swings compact and close to the body. This means that for each arm, the elbow should reach the side of the hip as the arm swings forward, followed by the hand reaching the side of the hip as the arm swings back. (see figure 10.5) The fingers are held together and the hands are kept open during running, cutting through the air like knives. The hands should never be clenched tightly, which creates excessive muscle tension in the hands and forearms.

Figure 10.12 **Chin up with eyes looking straight ahead.**

Figure 10.13 **Arms bent 90 degrees at the elbows.**

Connect and Correct: Establishing Overall Posture

The previously stated points help establish optimal positions of specific body regions for running. In addition, these body regions should be aligned with each other in a proper way.

Please examine figure 10.14*a* and *b* to understand correct whole-body posture. To conceptualize functional overall posture, a dot is placed in the

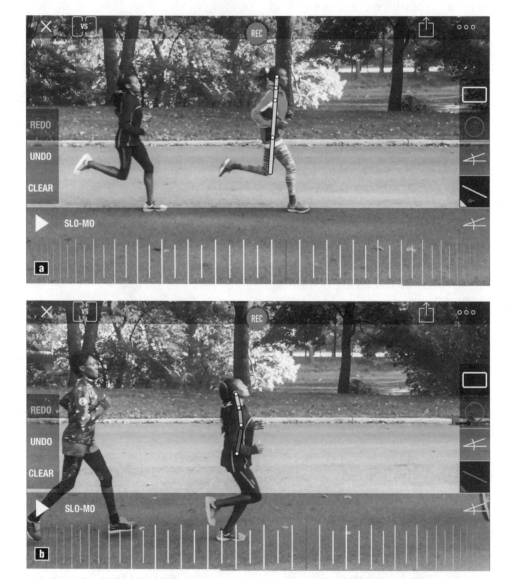

Figure 10.14 (*a*) To assess posture, dots placed in the center of the head, neck, thorax, and hips can be connected with straight lines. When posture is perfect, the three lines will form one continuous line. (*b*) When the dots do not line up, the resulting line develops a curve.

center of the head, the center of the neck, the center of the trunk, and the center of the hips. The dots are then connected by three lines.

The resulting three lines should form one straight line (not three lines at varying angles with each other)—that is, the line from the center of the hips to the center of the head should be straight and lie directly over the individually drawn lines. If this is not the case, one can correctly assume that there are postural problems, especially issues with a forward or backward inclination of the hips or head.

Using an effective and inexpensive application such as Coach's Eye, have a friend or colleague take video from the side while you are running. The app can then be used to create the four points described above (head, neck, trunk, and hips) and to draw the relevant lines Deliberate and specific adjustments in posture can then be made by the runner during subsequent training runs, with video retaken after several days to assess establishment of correct overall posture.

Summary

Posture is often neglected by runners, even though it plays a role in promoting fatigue resistance, heightening performance, and resisting injury. Using the cues provided in this chapter and video inspection of postural alignment with a simple and straightforward app, runners can progressively modify posture over time and thus run faster with a lower energetic cost (i.e., with enhanced running economy).

11

Putting It All Together

In this age of abused therapeutic use exemptions (TUEs), inappropriate use of prescription medications, illegal pre-race intravenous infusions, undetectable testosterone creams, EPO-induced red blood cell expansions, asthma medications prescribed for non-asthmatic runners, and thyroid hormones provided to athletes with trouble-free thyroids—all as part of an effort to artificially change a runner's physiology and make him stronger and faster—it is nice to know that there is one thing in running that can never be faked: running form. "You can fool an athlete's normal physiology with drugs and illegal performance-boosters, but you can never fake the physics of form," notes Walt Reynolds, a strength and conditioning specialist who has worked on running form with some of the world's best runners, including Cynthia Limo, Mary Wacera, and Monicah Ngige (1). There is no supplement or drug that will upgrade running form. Great form has to be learned and earned through the use of drills, form-specific exercises, and regular practice.

Optimal form will always be primarily determined by four key components of running gait: foot-strike pattern (FAT), reversal of swing (ROS, also known as "sweep"), shank angle at initial contact with the ground (SAT), and the ratio of reversal of swing to maximal shank angle (ROS/MSA). These four variables are the essentials, the form factors that determine whether a runner can reach her true potential and how likely she is to be injured. Most runners have these variables configured in sub-optimal ways, which results in a higher risk of injury and a decreased chance of reaching an optimal state of fitness and attaining the best possible personal records. This is true even when a runner seems to be running smoothly and her upper body mechanics appear flawless. When the four variables are combined in the right way, a runner can achieve her potential with the lowest possible risk of injury, even when the upper body is moving around with Zatopek-like jerks and shudders. This chapter will show you how to put together the four key components of form in the best way.

Foot-Strike Pattern

Even though about 95 percent of distance runners are heel-strikers (2, 3), it has become clear that a midfoot-strike pattern is superior to heel-striking. This is true from the standpoints of both performance and the likelihood of injury: Midfoot-strikers are simply faster and less likely to get hurt.

Looking at the matter from a performance standpoint, it is important to note that the fastest runners in the world—elite and super-elite sprinters—are forefoot-strikers, not heel-strikers. No world-class sprinter has ever been a heel-striker. In addition, the quickest distance runners in the world—the elite Kenyans and Ethiopians—are forefoot- and midfoot-strikers.

Why is this true? Why don't we see a mix of heel-, midfoot-, and forefoot-striking among the world's best runners? Until now, the explanation for this phenomenon has not been entirely clear. But thanks to recent research carried out at Southern Methodist University and Harvard University, we now know that the chain of events that occurs during the stance phase of gait (when propulsive forces are produced) is completely different when comparing heel-striking to midfoot-striking. Specifically, heel-striking places negative limits on force production, while midfoot-striking sets the stage for the optimal amount and timing of propulsive forces (4).

Traditionally the stance phase of gait, when all vertical and horizontal propulsive forces are actually produced, has been simplistically divided into three parts: initial contact with the ground, mid-stance (support), and toe-off. With this simplistic view of stance, it seemed to make little difference whether a runner initially hit the ground with the heel or with the middle of the foot.

Heel-Striking

However, the stance scenario is actually much more complex. If a runner is a heel-striker, the overall gait cycle proceeds in this order:

1. The still point of the foot, also known as the zero point, is reached. Still point is the moment when the foot, ankle, and lower part of the leg reach the farthest point forward during the swing phase of gait. The still point precedes ground contact and is the point at which MSA is measured.

2. After still point is reached, the foot moves downward and backward toward the ground and makes initial impact heel-first, usually on the lateral aspect of the heel with a typically large SAT.

3. As seen on the all-important graph illustrating ground-reaction force as a function of time during stance, a force equal to one times body weight is reached very quickly (figure 11.1).

4. On the graph illustrating force as a function of time during stance, a force equal to 1.5 times body weight is also reached extremely quickly when heel-striking is the preferred initial ground-contact option.

5. The first peak in vertical force is finally reached during stance (after Steps 3 and 4), followed by a small "trough" which represents a slight reduction in force.

6. After the first peak in force is reached, the shank finally assumes a vertical position, at a 90-degree angle with the ground. Up until this time, the shank has been inclined forward, relative to the body.

7. As the body moves forward over the foot, a second, higher peak in vertical propulsive force is attained.

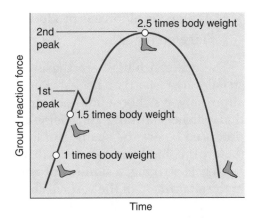

Figure 11.1 Force vs. time relationship for a heel-striker during stance. Note the very quick rise in impact force and the rapid attainment of a force equal to 1.5 times body weight.

8. Take-off from the ground finally occurs, and the runner is airborne.

Midfoot-Striking

When the midfoot-strike prevails, the stance phase of gait is usually shorter in duration, with the following steps occurring:

1. Zero point (still point) is reached, just as was the case with heel-striking.

2. The foot moves down and back and makes contact with the ground in the midfoot area (figure 11.2).

3. A vertical, 90-degree shank angle is reached prior to attainment of a ground-reaction force equal to one times body weight. Note the difference from the heel-strike pattern, in which vertical shank angle was not attained until after forces equal to 1 and 1.5 times body weight were reached.

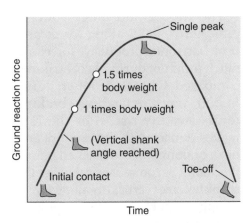

4. A force equal to one times body weight is attained as the body moves forward over the foot.

5. A force equal to 1.5 times body weight is reached as the body continues to move forward relative to the foot.

Figure 11.2 Force vs. time relationship for a midfoot-striker during stance. Note the less rigid rise in impact force (compared to heel-striking) and the attainment of a vertical shank angle before even one body weight of force is provided.

6. Peak vertical force is produced.

7. Take-off occurs.

The difference between these chains of events explains why midfoot-strikers are faster than heel-strikers, and why the best runners in the world almost always choose midfoot-striking over the heel-strike pattern. Note that with heel-striking, considerable amounts of vertical propulsive force are produced before the shank and leg reach a favorable mechanical position (before the shank reaches vertical), when force is pushing up and backward. With heel-striking, a significant amount of vertical force is produced prior to the attainment of the vertical shank and thus can only push the body up and back—since the shank angle is still positive when one times body weight and 1.5 times body weight are reached.

In contrast with a midfoot-strike, the large vertical forces of one and 1.5 times body weight are attained after the shank becomes vertical, when the leg is ready to push up and forward. Critical, vertical propulsive forces are produced too early and thus counter-productively and wastefully with the heel-strike pattern; on the other hand, with midfoot-landing, the major propulsive forces exert themselves at the proper time during stance.

Horizontal Forces

Horizontal braking forces resist the forward movement of the body, while horizontal propulsive forces promote the direct forward movement of the body. During stance, horizontal braking forces occurs first, immediately after ground contact, but eventually give way to horizontal propulsive forces as the stance phase proceeds. After the shank reaches a vertical (perpendicular) position with respect to the ground, horizontal braking forces disappear and horizontal propulsive forces progressively increase (figure 11.3).

The timing and magnitude of peak horizontal braking forces and peak horizontal propulsive forces are much different during heel-striking, compared with midfoot-striking. In both types of landings, braking forces steadily rise after the foot makes contact with the ground, and peak braking force is reached before the shank becomes vertical. After the shank becomes vertical, braking forces disappear and horizontal propulsive forces comes to the fore. This means that in order to minimize braking and to optimize forward propulsion

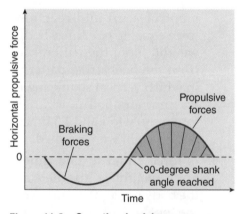

Figure 11.3 **Once the shank becomes perpendicular with the ground, horizontal braking forces end and horizontal propulsive forces begin.**

and thus speed, a runner should reach a vertical shank angle as quickly as possible during stance.

From the two step-by-step gait events described previously in this chapter (with heel-striking and midfoot-striking), it becomes obvious that peak braking force is reached later in stance with a heel-strike, compared with midfoot-striking, since vertical shank angle is attained later in stance. In other words, braking plays a larger role during stance when the landing strategy is heel-striking. With a midfoot-strike, a runner can move more quickly out of braking into horizontal propulsive force. This creates less total braking action and a quicker shift into horizontal forward propulsion when midfoot-striking is the preferred landing mode. When midfoot-landings are used, results can include shorter contact times (and thus higher step rates and running speeds) and greater forward-directed force.

Although rarely mentioned in popular running magazines, online articles, and books, a key goal of training for runners is to position the shank and leg in the proper way and shift the force-time curve up and to the left. In other words, the runner who is interested in increasing speed should produce larger propulsive forces (after the 90-degree shank angle has been reached) and produce those forces more quickly than before. This may appear to be a paradox, since we have already mentioned that higher loading rates of force (VALRs) increase the risk of injury. However, bear in mind that the ratio of VALR/running velocity is always lower in good-form runners, compared with heel-strikers. Thus, good-form runners can shift the force-time curve to the left with a lower risk of injury, because there is less risk that VALR will exceed a critical, injury producing level. The problem that poor-form (common-form) runners have is that they produce very high VALR values at slow speeds; when they try to move the force-time curve up and to the left (i.e., try to move faster), they create monumental, injury producing VALRs). For the good-form runner, moving the force-time curve up and to the left leads to longer step lengths, quicker step rates, and thus higher running velocities, both in training and competition. Compared with heel-striking, midfoot-landings are much superior in this regard (figure 11.4).

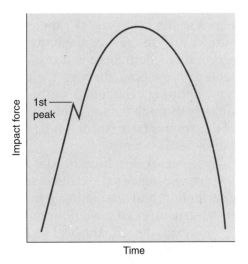

Figure 11.4 **One of the goals of form work is to shift the force-time curve up and to the left (i.e., to produce more propulsive force and to produce it more quickly. The good-from runner can do this with a low risk of injury because her ratio of VALR/running velocity is moderate [she can produce more speed with a lower VALR] and thus there is less risk of exceeding an injury producing threshold level of VALR).**

■ The Critical 10 Milliseconds

It's worth considering the "one-hundredth of a second effect." Studies have demonstrated that midfoot-strikers generally have stance durations that are about one-hundredth of a second (10 milliseconds) shorter per step, compared with the stances of heel-strikers. This may seem like a small effect, but the disparity can become sizable in race situations.

For example, take the case of a heel-striker who wants to break through the 40-minute barrier for the 10K. Let's say that she is taking 180 steps per minute and is currently capable of running the 10K in 41 minutes. In that time, she takes a total of $41 \times 180 = 7,380$ steps. If she shifts from heel-striking to midfoot-striking, she will save approximately $7,380 \times .01 = 73.8$ seconds, reducing her 10K finishing time to a very nice 39:46.2. Her time improvements in the half-marathon and marathon would be even greater. These time upgrades ignore the possible positive effects on step length when changing from heel- to midfoot-striking; the shift could lengthen steps also. (Remember that midfoot-strikes are more advantageous from the standpoint of the production of both vertical and horizontal propulsive forces.)

Effects of Foot-Strike Pattern on Injury

The human heel is a terrible shock absorber during the act of running. Two bones in the heel—the calcaneus and talus—stand between the running surface and the rest of the body. When the heel hits the ground, impact (ground-reaction) force is transmitted directly through the calcaneus and talus into the tibia, through the tibia to the knee, through the knee to the femur, through the femur to the hip, through the hip into the spine, and directly through the spine into the head. There is relatively little modulation of this impact force (shock), as it is transmitted directly and rapidly through the skeletal system.

By contrast, the human foot has 26 bones; 33 joints; and more than 100 muscles, tendons, and ligaments—all of which are capable of absorbing, distributing, and dissipating impact shock. When a midfoot-strike is chosen, these structures go to work to soften shock.

This explains why the heel-striker displays a rapidly developed, significant first peak in ground-reaction force on the force-time curve, a peak that is missing in the curve of the midfoot-striker. This first peak signifies the rapid increase in impact shock force experienced by the heel-striker. Various researchers have linked force-loading rate (the rate at which ground-reaction force increases after the foot makes contact with the ground, also called VALR for Vertical Average Loading Rate) to injury in runners (5, 6, 7). Force loading rate is higher in heel-strikers, compared with midfoot-strikers. Among runners, the higher the loading rate, the greater the risk of injury.

In running, the heel plays a key role, but that role is not intended to be shock absorption. The heel is poorly suited for absorbing shock and prefers to pass shock immediately "up the chain" into the rest of the body. The key role of the heel during stance is to provide proper stiffness, a variable that is strongly linked with running economy. But this stiffness has to be provided at the right time—not when the foot is making initial contact with the ground, which is when the stiffness will only help transfer shock up the leg to the knee, hip, spine, and head.

Shank Angle

Two shank angles are critically important: shank angle at initial impact (touchdown) with the ground (SAT), and shank angle at maximal vertical propulsive force (SAMVF). Among distance runners, SAT ranges from extremely positive (around 20 degrees, figure 11.5) to mildly positive (around five degrees, figure 11.6). The larger the positive SAT, the greater the braking force (and the duration of breaking force) during stance. Large shank angles also tend to be correlated with heel-striking, which promotes the sub-optimal magnitude and timing of force production. On the other hand, a negative shank angle increases the risk of falling and also decreases total vertical force production. Somewhat counter-intuitively, vertical force is a more important producer of speed, compared with horizontal force

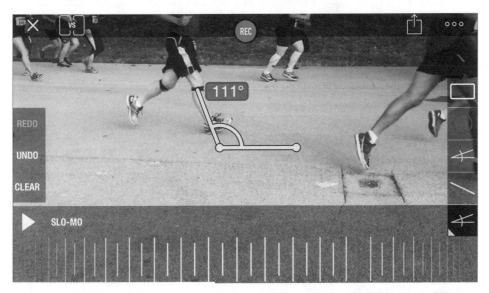

Figure 11.5 **Highly positive SATs lead to heel-striking, longer stance times, lower step rates, greater braking forces, higher impact-force loading rates and thus greater "breaking" forces, and poor timing of vertical propulsive forces.**

Figure 11.6 Slightly positive SATs lead to midfoot-striking, shorter stance times, higher step rates, reduced periods of braking forces, faster running speeds, smaller impact-force loading rates and thus lower "breaking" forces, and optimal timing of vertical propulsive force.

production. In fact, during very fast running, vertical force production can be 11 times greater than horizontal force production. It is entirely wrong to say, as many running publications are currently stating, that vertical forces are bad during running and should be minimized. The truth is that vertical forces are crucial. As a runner increases her vertical force production, her maximal running velocity and thus overall performances also increase. This is true for both sprinters and distance runners.

Video analysis of world-record performances at distances ranging from 100 meters all the way up to the marathon reveals that—in all cases except one—SAT falls within the range of a positive four to eight degrees (see tables 11.1 and 11.2). It is thus believed that optimal shank angle is within this range, probably close to six degrees. Astoundingly, the world-record holder in the 100 meters (Usain Bolt) and the world-record holder in the marathon (Dennis Kimetto) have very similar SATs: They both prefer seven-degree collisions, a similarity in form that is unlikely to be coincidence.

There is also an optimal negative shank angle associated with the highest-possible vertical ground-reaction force. A runner's maximum speed and her ability to generate vertical ground-reaction force are tightly linked. It appears from video analysis of a variety of runners that this shank angle occurs at about negative 23 degrees. This is an angle that is reached more quickly during midfoot-striking, compared with heel-striking. In addition, heel-strikers may produce maximum vertical propulsive force before this angle is reached—at a sub-optimal time.

TABLE 11.1

SATs for Men's World-Record Performances From 100 Meters to the Marathon

EVENT	RECORD	ATHLETE	SAT	MSA	NATIONALITY	DATE	ROS	MEET	LOCATION	ROS/SAT
100 m (progression)	9.58 (+0.9m/s)	Usain Bolt	+7°	27°	Jamaica	16 August 2009	+20°	World Championships	Berlin, Germany	2.86
200 m (progression)	19.19 (−0.3m/s)	Usain Bolt	+7°	27°	Jamaica	20 August 2009	+20°	World Championships	Berlin, Germany	2.86
400 m (progression)	43.18	Michael Johnson	+5°	22°	USA	26 August 1999	+17°	World Championships	Seville, Spain	3.40
800 m (progression)	1:40.91	David Rudisha	+7°	19°	Kenya	9 August 2012	+12°	Olympic Games	London, UK	1.71
1000 m (progression)	2:11.96	Noah Ngeny	+8°	18°	Kenya	5 September 1999	+10°	Rieti Meeting	Rieti, Italy	1.25
1500 m (progression)	3:26.00	Hicham El Guerrouj	+7°	18°	Morocco	14 July 1998	+11°	Golden Gala	Rome, Italy	1.57
Mile (progression)	3:43.13	Hicham El Guerrouj	+7°	18°	Morocco	7 July 1999	+11°	Golden Gala	Rome, Italy	1.57
2000 m (progression)	4:44.79	Hicham El Guerrouj	+7°	18°	Morocco	7 September 1999	+11°	ISTAF	Berlin, Germany	1.57
3000 m (progression)	7:20.67	Daniel Komen	+6°	16°	Kenya	1 September 1996	+10°	Rieti Meeting	Rieti, Italy	1.67
5000 m (progression)	12:37.35	Kenenisa Bekele	+8°	17°	Ethiopia	31 May 2004	+9°	Fanny Blankers-Koen Games	Hengelo, Netherlands	1.13
10,000 m (progression)	26:17.53	Kenenisa Bekele	+8°	17°	Ethiopia	26 August 2005	+9°	Memorial Van Damme	Brussels, Belgium	1.13

(continued)

145

TABLE 11.1 *(continued)*

EVENT	RECORD	ATHLETE	SAT	MSA	NATIONALITY	DATE	ROS	MEET	LOCATION	ROS/SAT
10 km (road)	26:44	Leonard Patrick Komon	+8°	19°	Kenya	26 September 2010	+11°	Singelloop	Utrecht, Netherlands	1.38
15 km (road)	41:13	Leonard Patrick Komon	+8°	19°	Kenya	21 November 2010	+11°	Zevenheuvelenloop	Nijmegen, Netherlands	1.38
20,000 m (track)	56:25.98+	Haile Gebrselassie	+8°	18°	Ethiopia	27 June 2007	+10°	Golden Spike Ostrava	Ostrava, Czech Republic	1.25
20 km (road)	55:21+	Zersenay Tadese	+6°	15°	Eritrea	21 March 2010	+9°	Lisbon Half Marathon	Lisbon, Portugal	1.50
Half marathon (progression)	58.23	Zersenay Tadese	+6°	15°	Eritrea	21 March 2010	+9°	Lisbon Half Marathon	Lisbon, Portugal	1.50
One hour (progression)	21,285 m	Haile Gebrselassie	+8°	18°	Ethiopia	27 June 2007	+10°	Golden Spike Ostrava	Ostrava, Czech Republic	1.25
25,000 m (track)	1:12:25.4+	Moses Mosop	+7°	16°	Kenya	3 June 2011	+9°	Prefontaine Classic	Eugene, OR, USA	1.29

Event	Time	Athlete			Country	Date		Competition	Location	
25 km (road)	1:11.18	Dennis Kipruto Kimetto	+8°	16°	Kenya	6 May 2012	+8°	Big 25	Berlin, Germany	1.00
30,000 m (track)	1:26:47.4	Moses Mosop	+7°	16°	Kenya	3 June 2011	+9°	Prefontaine Classic	Eugene, OR, USA	1.29
30 km (road)	1:27:38+	Patrick Makau Musyoki	+5°	22°	Kenya	25 September 2011	+17°	Berlin Marathon	Berlin, Germany	3.40
Marathon (progression)	2:02:57	Dennis Kipruto Kimetto	+8°	16°	Kenya	28 September 2014	+8°	Berlin Marathon	Berlin, Germany	1.00
	2:03:23	Wilson Kipsang	+5°	14°	Kenya	29 September 2013	+9°	Berlin Marathon	Berlin, Germany	1.80
	2:03:02	Geoffrey Mutai	+3°	12°	Kenya	18 April 2011	+9°	Boston Marathon	Boston, USA	3.00
3000 m (steeplechase)	7:53.63	Saif Saaeed Shaheen	+8°	17°	Qatar	3 September 2004	+9°	Memorial Van Damme	Brussels, Belgium	1.13

Legend: Shaded areas are awaiting ratification as of press time.

TABLE 11.2

SATs for Women's World-Record Performances From 100 Meters to the Marathon

EVENT	RECORD	ATHLETE	SAT	MSA	NATIONALITY	DATE	ROS	MEET	LOCATION
100 m (progression)	10.49 (0.0 m/s)	Florence Griffith Joyner	+12°	33°	USA	16 July 1988	+21°	US Olympic Trials	Indianapolis, IN, USA
200 m (progression)	21.34 (+1.3 m/s)	Florence Griffith Joyner	+10°	32°	USA	29 September 1988	+22°	Olympic Games	Seoul, South Korea
400 m (progression)	47.60	Marita Koch	+6°	17°	East Germany	6 October 1985	+11°	World Cup	Canberra, Australia
800 m (progression)	1:53.28	Jarmila Kratochvílová	+8°	18°	Czechoslovakia	26 July 1983	+10°		Munich, West Germany
1000 m (progression)	2:28.98	Svetlana Masterkova	+7°	22°	Russia	23 August 1996	+15°	Memorial Van Damme	Brussels, Belgium
1500 m (progression)	3:50.46	Qu Yunxia	+9°	19°	China	11 September 1993	+10°	Chinese National Games	Beijing, PR China
Mile (progression)	4:12.56	Svetlana Masterkova	+7°	22°	Russia	14 August 1996	+15°	Weltklasse Zürich	Zürich, Switzerland
2000 m	5:25.36	Sonia O'Sullivan	+10°	25°	Ireland	8 July 1994	+15°		Edinburgh, Scotland, UK
3000 m (progression)	8:06.11	Wang Junxia	+9°	19°	China	13 September 1993	+10°	Chinese National Games	Beijing, PR China
5000 m (progression)	14:11.15	Tirunesh Dibaba	+8°	18°	Ethiopia	15 November 2009	+10°	Zevenheuvelenloop	Nijmegen, Netherlands

Event	Time	Athlete			Country	Date		Competition	Location
10,000 m (progression)	29:31.78	Wang Junxia	+9°	19°	China	8 September 1993	+10°	Chinese National Games	Beijing, PR China
10 km (road)	30:21	Paula Radcliffe	+6°	18°	Great Britain	23 February 2003	+12°	World's Best 10K	San Juan, Puerto Rico
15 km (road)	46:27.7	Tirunesh Dibaba	+8°	18°	Ethiopia	15 November 2009	+10°	Zevenheuvelenloop	Nijmegen, Netherlands
20,000 m (track)	1:05:26.6	Tegla Loroupe	+9°	15°	Kenya	3 September 2000	+6°		Borgholzhausen, Germany
20 km (road)	1:01:56+	Florence Kiplagat	+9°	18°	Kenya	16 February 2014	+9°	Barcelona Half Marathon	Barcelona, Spain
Half marathon (progression)	1:05:12	Florence Kiplagat	+9°	18°	Kenya	16 February 2014	+9°	Barcelona Half Marathon	Barcelona, Spain
25,000 m (track)	1:27:05.84	Tegla Loroupe	+9°	15°	Kenya	21 September 2002	+6°		Mengerskirchen, Germany
25 km (road)	1:19.53	Mary Keitany	+9°	18°	Kenya	9 May 2010	+9°	Big 25	Berlin, Germany
30,000 m (track)	1:45:50.00	Tegla Loroupe	+9°	15°	Kenya	7 June 2003	+6°		Warstein, Germany
30 km (road)	1:38:23+	Liliya Shobukhova	n/a	22°	Russia	9 October 2011	n/a	Chicago Marathon	Chicago, USA
	1:36:36+	Paula Radcliffe	+6°	18°	Great Britain	13 April 2003	+12°	London Marathon	London, UK
Marathon (progression)	2:15:25	Paula Radcliffe	+6°	18°	Great Britain	13 April 2003	+12°	London Marathon	London, UK
3000 m (steeplechase)	8:58.81	Gulnara Samitova-Galkina	+10°	22°	Russia	17 August 2008	+12°	Olympic Games	Beijing, PR China

Reversal of Swing

Reversal of swing (ROS) is the change in shank angle that occurs between the still point (zero point, MSA) and initial contact with the running surface. During running, ROS has three functions:

1. It can optimize SAT by moving the shank and foot into the correct position (with about a six-degree SAT).
2. It can improve "punch," or the force with which the foot and leg strike the ground at the end of ROS. Greater punch translates directly into higher vertical propulsive forces. Longer, higher-velocity sweeps improve punch, while abridged, sluggish sweeps diminish it.
3. If small, it increases the chances that the foot is landing in a position too far ahead of the body. This increases horizontal braking forces and directs vertical propulsive forces upward and backward.

For comparative purposes, it is important to note that a runner like Usain Bolt has a zero point of about 27 degrees (on average) and an SAT of around 7 degrees, yielding an ROS of about 20 degrees and providing a tremendous amount of punch on the ground (figure 11.7). Dennis Kimetto has a zero point of about 14 degrees and an SAT of roughly seven degrees, yielding an ROS of seven degrees (figure 11.8).

Kyodo News via Getty Images

Figure 11.7 **ROS for Bolt is about 20.**

By contrast, the average distance runner has a zero point (MSA) of around 18 degrees and an SAT of 16 degrees, yielding a minuscule and counter-productive ROS of only two degrees—with all the negative consequences associated with such a paltry amount of movement. With this kind of form, there is almost zero productive punch against the ground, horizontal braking forces are prolonged and maximized, and vertical propulsive forces are directed upward and backward. Fortunately, as this book explains, ROS and SAT are highly trainable.

Ratio of ROS to Maximum Shank Angle (ROS/MSA)

One final form variable is extremely important: the ratio of ROS to the shank angle at zero point (MSA), which we can call the "golden ratio" (ROS/MSA). This ratio ties together two critical variables—the zero point and SAT—and thus provides a great deal of information about a runner's form, just as $v\dot{V}O_2max$ reveals more about an athlete's running capacity than $\dot{V}O_2max$ alone. ($\dot{V}O_2max$ is a runner's maximal aerobic capacity, but $v\dot{V}O_2max$ is a runner's actual running velocity when $\dot{V}O_2max$ is attained, which is a more valuable piece of information.)

As mentioned earlier, Usain Bolt has a typical MSA of about 27 degrees and an SAT of 7 degrees, yielding an ROS of 20 degrees. Thus, his ratio, ROS/MSA is roughly 20/27 or .74. Dennis Kimetto has a ratio of 7/14, or .5, reflecting the slower running speed required for the marathon and thus a lower dependence on a powerful punch. In contrast, the average distance runner who is attempting to run quickly has an MSA of 18 degrees, an SAT of 16 degrees, and thus an ROS of only two degrees. That creates a disastrous ratio of 2/18 = .11 This is the ratio used by Bolt and Kimetto when they are in full braking mode—when they are trying to stop!

The ratio of ROS/MSA can vary widely among runners, but video analysis of the world's best sprinters reveals that the ratio always falls in the range of about .7 to .75. Video analysis of the world's best distance runners demonstrates that the ratio is always within a range of .5 to .75. During Eliud Kipchoge's 2017 attempt to break the two-hour time barrier for the marathon (when he ran 2:00:24), his ratio was consistently close to .7. Video analysis of the common-form runner shows a ratio in the range of .1 to .2. The ratio of ROS/MSA is key, reflecting the quality of both a runner's ROS and the way in which she interacts with the ground, and yet it is completely ignored by most coaches and runners. Like its components, ROS and SAT, the ratio is highly trainable, and improvements in the ratio can lead to huge gains in running performance. Runners can develop the capacity to punch the ground more powerfully, and yet with less risk of injury.

Summary

Every serious runner wants to improve speed. Unfortunately, few serious runners are working on changing FAT, SAT, ROS, and ROS/MSA, let alone changing them in the directions that are actually necessary to boost speed. (In fact, most runners are completely unaware of these critical variables.) Runners are usually focused on improving the capacities of the heart and muscles only, which is akin to fine-tuning the engine of a high-quality car and then outfitting the vehicle with square wheels. Only when runners' highly developed physical capacities are matched with the optimization of all the key form variables can runners attain their highest-possible performances.

References

1. Walt Reynolds, personal communication, April 7, 2017

2. M.O. de Almeida et al., "Is the Rearfoot Pattern the Most Frequent Foot Strike Pattern Among Recreational Shod Distance Runners?" *Physical Therapy and Sport,* e-published (accessed February 24, 2014). doi: 10.1016/j.ptsp.2014.02.005. Epub 2014 Feb 26.

3. M.E. Kasmer et al., "Foot-Strike Pattern and Performance in a Marathon," *International Journal of Sports, Physiology, and Performance* 8, no. 3 (2013): 286–292.

4. W. Reynolds. "Midfoot Landings and the Production of Propulsive Forces During Running," www.runhackers.com (accessed December 7, 2016).

5. H.P. Crowell and I.S. David, "Gait Retraining to Reduce Lower Extremity Loading in Runners," *Clinical Biomechanics* 26 (2011): 78–83.

6. A.I. Daoud et al., "Foot Strike and Injury Rates in Endurance Runners: A Retrospective Study," *Medicine & Science in Sports & Exercise* 44, no. 7 (2012): 1325–1334.

7. I.S. Davis, B.J. Bowser, and D.R. Mullineaux, "Greater Vertical Impact Loading in Female Runners With Medically Diagnosed Injuries: A Prospective Investigation," *British Journal of Sports Medicine,* http://bjsm.bmj.com (accessed April 1, 2016).

PART
III

Form Factors for Running Success

Running Shoes and Form

When you wake up in the morning and slip into your running shoes in preparation for a run, you have unknowingly changed your running form in a significant way without even taking your first step out the door. That's because research reveals that running shoes have a profound effect on form. Compared with sauntering out the door barefooted or in minimal running shoes, traditional running shoes with elevated, cushioned heels steer you toward the following gait patterns.

Pattern A: Impact Transient

In traditional running shoes, a runner maximizes the "impact transient" (an abrupt collision force acting on the leg during the first 50 milliseconds of stance after the foot hits the ground), compared with barefoot running or running in minimal shoes. The magnitude of the impact transient is three times greater in traditional running shoes, compared with unshod running. In other words, your running shoes, thought to protect you from the impact forces of running, can actually increase the impact forces (1) (figure 12.1).

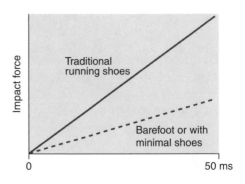

Pattern B: Heel Strike

In traditional running shoes, the ankle is less plantar-flexed each time the foot hits the ground. This means that a runner is much more likely to make initial contact with the ground with the rear portion of the foot,

Figure 12.1 Running in conventional shoes is associated with a dramatic impact transient— a powerfully increasing impact force moving up the leg during the first 50 milliseconds of stance.

instead of the front area (in other words, the runner would be running with a rearfoot or heel-strike pattern) (2) (figure 12.2).

Figure 12.2 The modern running shoe tends to steer runners away from (a) a more natural unshod landing pattern on the ground, and toward (b) a landing pattern that features a dorsiflexed ankle and a ground strike on the rear portion of the foot.

Pattern C: Knee Angle

In traditional running shoes, the knee is almost always less flexed at ground contact, meaning that the runner is hitting the ground with a significantly straighter leg, compared with running barefooted or in minimal shoes (3). The "knee angle" (the angle made by the posterior portions of the thigh and calf) for almost all runners wearing traditional, heel-elevated shoes is consistently in the range of 166 to 180 degrees at ground contact (4) (figure 12.3a).

By contrast, knee angles for barefooted runners, athletes wearing minimal running shoes with non-elevated heels, and runners who have carried out the running-form drills outlined in this book, fall within the range of 148 to 158 degrees for middle-distance and distance runners and 158 to 166 degrees for sprinters at ground contact (5) (figure 12.3b).

Landing on the heel with the ankle dorsi-flexed and a straight leg is responsible for the heightened impact transient in thick-heeled, traditional running shoes. If this is difficult to understand, think for a moment of the

Figure 12.3 (*a*) In traditional shoes, the knee angle is larger at impact with the ground, meaning that the leg is straighter. (*b*) For the barefoot runner or the runner in minimal shoes, the knee angle is less at the moment of impact, meaning that the knee is less straight (the knee is more flexed).

leg as being an iron pole that strikes the ground at high speed. Contrast that with an elastic appendage that can bend and store energy at its base (the foot), near its bottom (the ankle) and also at its middle (the knee). During the first 50 milliseconds after impact with the ground, which of these two structures would experience the greatest impact force in its top region (the end of the structure farthest from the ground)? It seems obvious that the knee, hip, and thus the spine would take greater, destructive poundings in traditional shoes, compared with running barefooted or the use of minimal shoes.

Impact Forces in Heel-Strikers

When a runner lands on the ground with his heel and a straight (or nearly straight) leg, the force of impact is transmitted extremely rapidly, straight through the heel (which cannot store energy by flexing as the ankle does), straight through the unflexed knee and ramrod-straight leg, and then through the hip to the spine and thus all the way to the head. A pronounced heel-first landing sets off a chain reaction of shock transmission throughout the entire body. This chain of events begins with a sledgehammer-like impact on the posterior aspect of the calcaneus (heel bone) and progresses nearly instantaneously through the leg, hip, and upper body. Research reveals that the sledgehammer landings are not effectively moderated by the high, foamy heels of traditional shoes (in fact, the impact transient can be three times greater in such shoes).

When the heel strikes the ground during a rearfoot-strike, the impact shock force moves upward in the following way:

1. From the initial hammer strike on the calcaneus, up through the talus via the subtalar joint (figure 12.4)

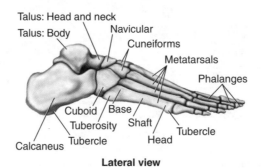

Lateral view

Figure 12.4   **With a heel strike, impact force is transmitted quickly through the calcaneus and talus into the tibia.**

2. From the talus into the tibia (shin bone) via the tibio-talar joint

3. From the tibia directly into the femur (thigh bone) by means of the tibio-femoral joint

4. From the femur into the pelvis (hip) via the acetabulo-femoral joint

5. From the pelvis into the vertebral column (spine) via the sacroiliac joint

6. From the spine into the cranium via the cranio-vertebral joint (figure 12.5)

The calcaneus is neither positioned nor structured to store and release energy by elastically flexing and recoiling after impact with the ground. As a result, the shock force of landing is transmitted straight up the body to the head in milliseconds. This brutal scenario occurs about 7,000 times during a simple run of 5 miles (or 8 kilometers); it is a key reason why at least 65 percent of runners (and 90 percent of marathon trainees) experience a running-related injury in any given year (remember that 95 percent of runners are heel-strikers) (6). The fast transmission of impact shock with rearfoot-striking is especially troubling when one considers the relatively poor functional strength of the legs in many runners.

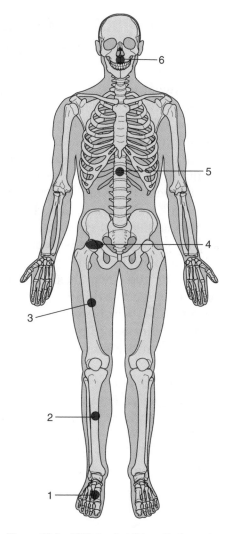

Figure 12.5 **With heel-striking, the impact transient is magnified and impact forces travel quickly up the skeletal chain to the head.**

Impact Absorption in Midfoot- and Forefoot-Strikers

Contrast what happens with heel-striking with what takes place during midfoot-striking. When a midfoot-landing occurs, the initial force of impact is taken on by the phalanges, metatarsals, cuneiforms, navicular bone, and cuboid bones—and the muscles and connective tissues in the joints in between them (figure 12.4). This is no small matter. Not counting the talus and calcaneus, there are 24 bones in the foot, along with about 30 joints between them and nearly 100 muscles, tendons, and ligaments. The foot is like a web of shock-absorbing structures, shaped by natural selection to accommodate and enhance running and walking, and it is this force-dissipating network that is bypassed when a runner chooses to crash into the ground with his heel.

The foot's two key arches (longitudinal and transverse) play an extraordinary assisting role during midfoot-strikes, not only supporting the bones of the foot and their related connective tissues and muscles, but also absorbing impact shocks and balancing the body (figure 12.6). The actions of the foot's arches and numerous joints explain why the impact force reaching the calcaneus and ankle is greatly reduced after a forefoot- or midfoot-impact, compared with a hammer-like heel strike.

In addition, when a runner hits the ground with a compliant, plantar-flexed ankle and also with a compliant, flexed knee, much of the impact force is stored productively in the ankle and knee, instead of being passed "up the chain" to the head as a damaging shock force. The word "productively" is used here because the force of impact—which dorsi-flexes the initially

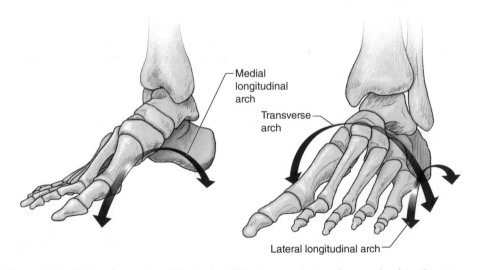

Figure 12.6 The two key arches of the foot mollify, store, and return force and reduce the magnitude of the impact transient.

plantar-flexed ankle and flexes the knee even further—stretches the muscles, tendons, and ligaments at those joints (effectively storing "elastic energy" in the joints). When these muscles snap back elastically to their unstretched positions, they provide "no-cost" (energy expenditure free) propulsive force which drives a runner forward.

Effects of Thick Heels on Form

With traditional running shoes, your cadence automatically decreases because you take fewer steps per minute as you run, compared with running barefooted or in minimal shoes. This cadence reduction can have a very negative impact on running velocity, which depends entirely on step rate and step length. Traditional shoes tend to decrease step rate by expanding time spent on the ground per step by about .01 seconds. For each 180 steps (expenditure free energy), this can keep a runner on the ground for an extra 1.8 seconds, thus causing running velocity to decline.

Why do traditional running shoes have such a corrupting impact on running form? One of the most glaring problems associated with the traditional running shoe is the presence of extra midsole material in the heel, which elevates the heel above the rest of the foot. In fact, there is about a .5-inch (or 12-millimeter) differential between the heel and forefoot in many conventional running shoes. This additional padding in the heel area is often believed to enhance shock absorption and therefore limit the risk of injury, even though injury rates have not improved since the 1970s when heel-elevated running shoes were introduced (figure 12.7). In fact, many runners actually select shoes on the basis of heel height, believing that heel-elevated shoes, with their excess of foamy material in the rear portions of the shoes, produce softer landings with the ground on each step. Running shoe companies often tout their big-heeled shoes as providing superior "cushioning" for the runner who needs a "softer ride."

A key problem with all of this is that heel-elevated shoes are actually associated with greater impact transients, compared with "zero-drop" shoes (which by definition have no difference between the height of the heel and the front part of the shoe). Runners who wear heel-elevated running shoes almost universally make the first impact with the ground on their heels, with each step as they run. Research has revealed that about 90 to 95 percent of runners clad in conventional running shoes are heel-

Figure 12.7 Thick-heeled running shoes lead to a number of very bad running-form habits, including heel-striking and landing on the ground with a straight leg and high SAT (and thus lousy "golden ratio").

strikers (7). The result is an impact transient that is three times greater, compared with midfoot-striking while running in minimal shoes or while barefoot.

Footwear Lessons From Kenya

Demonstrating that it is the shoes themselves that produce this effect, individuals who wear zero-drop shoes are much more likely to use a midfoot-strike pattern with the ground, and individuals who run barefoot rarely strike the ground with their heels first.

In countries where young runners tend to run barefoot and only later make a transition to shod running (usually in their mid-teen years), the change in footwear almost always corresponds with an alteration in running form. I have taken photos and videos of numerous Kenyan young people ranging in age from five to 13 and noted a consistent pattern: When these young runners move along barefoot, they strike the ground consistently with a midfoot-landing pattern. Close to 100 percent of the young runners one can observe in the Kenyan countryside are midfoot-strikers (figure 12.8).

By contrast, Kenyan runners in their late teens and older have usually acquired conventional running shoes, and consequently the frequency of midfoot-striking has dropped significantly. I have travelled to Kenya on 25 occasions and have taken many hours of video of Kenyan runners. By my estimates, the frequency of midfoot-striking has dropped from universality (when barefoot) to around 50 to 60 percent in well-trained, shod Kenyan harriers.

Interestingly enough, when the young, usually barefoot Kenyan runners slip on running shoes for the first time, they almost instantly become heel-strikers (figure 12.9).

Figure 12.8 **Individuals who run barefooted almost universally rely on a midfoot landing pattern**

Figure 12.9 **When these same runners slip on running shoes, they instantly become heel-strikers.**

A Host of Shoe-Related Form Problems

This pernicious effect of running shoes on foot-strike patterns leads to a number of problems, detailed on the pages that follow.

Increased Impact Transient

As mentioned, the heel-strike induced by cushioned, heel-elevated shoes actually increases the magnitude of the impact transient, instead of lessening it. This appears to be paradoxical because during heel-striking a runner is landing on the "softest," most-cushioned portion of the shoe. However, the mattress-like landings limit proprioception and thus may not initiate feedback loops in the nervous system which attenuate shock. Feedback loops diminish shock and usually involve greater ankle plantar flexion and knee flexion at impact with the ground, both of which soften the impact blow. In addition, a heel-strike, while it indeed involves landing on the mattress-like heel of the traditional running shoe, nonetheless bypasses the force-dissipating structures in the front of the foot.

Increased Force Rate

Heel-striking, compared with forefoot-striking, increases the rate at which force travels up the legs and through the body. This is because the heel-landings bypass the front areas of the feet and are associated with dorsi-flexed ankles and straight legs that are not flexed at the knee; thus there are no anatomical configurations in place to mollify force as it travels up the leg after impact.

Excess Shank Angle

Heel-striking is usually linked with a straight leg at impact with the ground and, on average, an SAT in excess of 14 degrees (figure 12.10). This leads to the production of extremely high shock transmission and braking forces after contact with the ground is made.

Increased Vertical Forces

A high SAT yields vertical ground reaction forces that reach one times body weight and 1.5 times body weight while the shank angle is still positive (before the shank has achieved a vertical position for the

Figure 12.10 **Runners who wear traditional, high-heeled shoes tend to have excessively high SATs.**

first time during stance). This means that a huge amount of vertical force is funneled into braking—rather than forward movement—since the forces are directed upward and backward, instead of upward and forward.

Although the relationship is never mentioned in popular running publications and books, the moment during gait when vertical impact force reaches 1.5 times body weight is actually a critical form variable and an excellent predictor of overall form. If you can measure a runner's shank angle at 1.5 times body weight, you can immediately tell if he has good form or not!

For example, take the case of a midfoot-striker who hits the ground with an initial shank angle of six degrees, compared with a heel-striker who touches down with an initial shank angle of 15 degrees. From the moment of touchdown, the ground reaction force increases as the shank and foot move backward in relation to the rest of the body. Eventually, the ground reaction force reaches 1.5 times body weight. At that point, the difference in shank angles is even greater between the midfoot- and heel-striker—much greater than the initial nine degrees. This is because the rate of force development is so much greater when the SAT is high and contact with the ground is achieved via heel-striking.

In fact, in almost every case of heel-striking, the shank angle is positive (the foot is ahead of the body) when a force of 1.5 times body weight is attained. In contrast, in almost every case of midfoot-striking, that 1.5 times body weight is reached at a negative shin angle, with the foot behind the body.

As a runner, when would you want to produce a significant propulsive force against the ground of 1.5 times your body weight: When your shank angle is positive and you are exerting braking, upward and backward forces on the ground, or when your shank angle is negative (with the foot behind the body) and you are exerting propulsive, upward, and forward forces against the ground? The position of the shank at 1.5 times body weight reveals overall running form and the potential to run quickly.

The thick heel of the modern running shoe leads to heel-striking on a nearly straight leg with a large SAT, which then leads to "braking and breaking effects." With the foot so far ahead of the body, braking forces are maximized. With the landing occurring on the heel, the rate at which impact forces are loaded into the leg increases, and the forces travel directly through the heel—untempered by the foot and ankle—and then through the ankle, shin, knee, upper portion of the leg, hip, spine, and head.

The heel-striking induced by the significantly elevated heel in the modern running shoe also lengthens the duration of the stance phase of gait, compared with forefoot-striking. The extent of this elongation can vary, but an average increase in time spent on the ground with heel-striking is about .01 seconds. This may seem quite small, but bear in mind that for the heel-striking runner taking 180 steps per minute and running one mile in six minutes, she would have $180 \times .01 \times 6 = 10.8$ seconds of wasted time built into the mile. With a midfoot-strike and thus without the extra .01 second per step, she would have the potential to clip off a mile in just 5:49.2 as a result of the change in form, without the need for further arduous training.

To summarize, heel-elevated shoes strongly encourage heel-striking. Heel-striking forces a runner to spend more time on the ground per step; produces more physical damage with each step; and leads to greater braking forces, diminished productive propulsive forces, and slower running speeds.

Other Effects of Shoes on Form

In addition to causing heel-striking, traditional running shoes have other significant effects on form. For example, such shoes tend to increase maximal shank angle (MSA) at still point (the point at which a foot reaches it farthest forward progress during swing, relative to the rest of the body). After MSA is reached, most conventional running shoes decrease reversal of swing (ROS, or the extent and magnitude of the subsequent downward and backward sweep of the foot toward the ground before landing). The lofty MSA and small ROS translate into a very high and sub-optimal SAT of approximately 14 to 20 degrees for the average distance runner—compared with two to six degrees in barefoot runners and individuals running in minimal shoes. This leads to the production of unnecessarily high braking forces during the stance phase of gait. The large MSA at still point is part of a runner's unwitting preparation for a heel-landing, which is tightly linked with the wearing of heel-elevated shoes.

Overall, traditional running shoes are associated with the following form characteristics:

- Higher SAT (because the runner is thrusting the shank forward to prepare for a heel-landing)
- A longer time period to reach a vertical shank during stance (because of the overly forward position of the foot at initial impact) and thus greater braking forces during stance
- An inability to place the shank in an optimal position for maximal vertical propulsive force (with traditional shoes, the foot is too far forward and the shank angle is too positive when the first peak in impact force is attained during stance)
- Less-economical movement—in part because of the reduction in elastic energy storage and release that is linked with heel-strikes; also because the foamy midsole of the traditional shoe is simply not as good at storing and returning energy as the human foot and also because the traditional shoe introduces an unstable platform on which the foot is perched (with this instability necessarily corrected by energy-consuming neuromuscular mechanisms)

It's important to note that transitioning from thick-soled traditional shoes to shoes with more minimal midsoles (also called *minimalist shoes*) is a good idea for many runners, but it is not without its perils. Changing from battleship-soled shoes to minimal models tends to result in a change from a heel-striking foot-strike pattern to midfoot contact. (Without a huge mattress at the heel end of the shoe, heel-striking suddenly begins to feel very uncomfortable.)

Midfoot-striking is desirable over the long term, of course, but a sudden shift from 30 weekly miles of heel-strike running to 30 miles of midfoot-striking is a recipe for disaster. The metatarsals of the feet and associated connective tissues will not be accustomed to directly absorbing the impact forces of running 90 times per minute per foot (given a cadence of 180)—a task that had been undertaken by the heels in thick-soled shoes. The abruptly elevated workloads placed on the metatarsals can produce foot pain, edema, inflammation in the metatarsals, and even stress fractures.

Furthermore, the Achilles tendon and calf muscles do significantly more work per step when midfoot-striking is in play. This is because the calf complex has to control ankle dorsiflexion after each contact with the ground and is stretched dynamically while contracting, a proven formula for muscle damage, soreness, and tightness. (During heel-striking, the calves don't have to control dorsiflexion, because the ankle is already dorsiflexed at ground contact and thus undergoes plantar flexion, placing stress on the shins.) This is why runners who shift from traditional shoes to minimal models and then go out for a 10-mile run often awake the following morning with excruciatingly painful calves.

What should be done to prevent the foot and calf damage associated with the shift from big-soled brogans to minimalist running shoes? Obviously, the answer is not to keep running with heel-strikes in the minimalist models. Rather, running volume (mileage) should be reduced drastically during the first few weeks of wearing the minimal shoes. Fitness can be maintained with the use of intense non-injury-producing cross-training (biking, swimming, rowing, etc.). A reasonable adjustment would be to reduce running-training volume to 20 percent of normal during the first week of minimal-shoe usage, with no long runs (greater than five miles) carried out in the minimal models. Successive weeks could then build to 40, 60, 80, and finally 100 percent of the usual training load. Thus it should take about a month before the usual training levels are resumed after the initiation of minimal-shoe usage.

Pronation and Supination

Runners sometimes hear that certain traditional shoes provide excellent control of pronation (inward rolling of the ankle) and supination (outward rolling of the ankle) during the stance phase of gait and thus furnish protection against injury. It is sometimes argued, for example, that such inward or outward actions can produce unusual torquing actions on the knee, increasing the risk of knee discomfort and damage. The implication of this kind of thinking would then be that minimal shoes increase the risk of knee injury, because they do not have the special features of the shoe models that allegedly control pronation and supination and thus keep the knees safe.

Such contentions are absurd. First, there is little evidence to support the notion that specific traditional shoes limit pronation and supination. In fact, because traditional shoes feature a high midsole platform, they are inherently unstable in medial and lateral directions, thus spiking pronation and supination. This is why you should never wear traditional running shoes while playing tennis, for example: If you move aggressively around the court, you would be at high risk of blowing out an ankle or a knee.

Second, there is little convincing scientific evidence to suggest that runners who pronate or supinate to an above-average extent have a higher risk of getting hurt. Rather, science continues to point out the key causes of running injury: 1. heel-striking and thus a lofty VALR (vertical average loading rate), 2. lack of running-specific strength, 3. overtraining, 4. poor recovery between workouts, and 5. a previous injury (about half of running injuries are simply re-occurrences of a previous problem).

Summary

The negative effects of running shoes on form can be changed. The truth is that a runner can run with good form in nearly any kind of shoe—traditional or minimal—and also barefoot. It is simply harder for a runner to do so with traditional, heel-elevated shoes, unless he is fully aware of the nature of good form and relentlessly conducts the proper form drills. Traditional, heel-elevated shoes tend to steer runners toward poor form practices. Instead of promoting stability, protecting against impact forces, and enhancing running economy, they tend to do exactly the opposite.

References

1. D.E. Lieberman et al., "Foot Strike Patterns and Collision Forces in Habitually Barefoot Versus Shod Runners," *Nature*, 463 (2009), 531–535.

2. Ibid.

3. Ibid.

4. Walter Reynolds, personal observation from "Good-Form Running" Instructional Sessions in Lansing, Michigan (2012–2017).

5. Ibid.

6. I.S. Davis et al., "Greater Vertical Impact Loading in Female Runners With Medically Diagnosed Injuries: A Prospective Investigation," *British Journal of Sports Medicine*, http://bjsm.bmj.com (accessed April 1, 2016).

7. D.E. Lieberman et al., "Variation in Foot Strike Patterns Among Habitually Barefoot and Shod Runners in Kenya," *PLOS ONE*, https://doi.org/10.1371/journal.pone.0131354 (2015).

13

Form Considerations for Special Groups

Runners commonly believe that each person has his own unique running style, perfectly suited to his individual neuromuscular and anatomical characteristics—and thus that he should be left relatively unperturbed by the general form recommendations made by exercise scientists and coaches. Unfortunately, this popular maxim exists far outside the domain of truth, as the laws of physics apply to all runners and do not vary by individual. The problem of form is a matter of resolving how best to control the collision between body and ground during gait—a repeated encounter that is governed by immutable physical truths. In the end, the runner's task is to develop form in a way that minimizes the risk of injury and—for those who are concerned with speed—improves the ability to run quickly. Expressed another way, the goal of running-form improvement is to optimize the production of propulsive force during running.

There may be 50 million everyday runners in the United States, but there are not 50 million ways to optimize form. Rather, there is a basic method for form that can be tweaked by unique groups of runners. For example, a runner who wants to be an elite sprinter may land on the ground with the same shank angle as the elite distance athlete (and even the non-elite, good-form distance runner). However, maximum shank angle (MSA) and reversal of swing (ROS) should be expanded significantly for the sprinter, compared with the distance-athlete's efforts. In this chapter, we will take a closer look at how form varies across different groups of runners and how a runner must change her form if she wants to belong to a certain group of athletes (for example, if she has aspirations to be an injury-free runner or an elite competitor).

The Elite Distance Runner

While form varies tremendously among distance runners as a whole, there is much less variation in form among truly elite distance runners (for example, those who appear on the IAAF top-50 list at various distances). A recent study determined that top-level elite distance runners eschew heel-striking and use forefoot- to midfoot-striking patterns (1). Elite athletes also run with a very similar MSA, ROS, SAT, and thus ROS/MSA ratio.

Elite distance runners who set world records, win world championships, and garner Olympic medals at distances of 5 kilometers and longer share the following key form characteristics:

- During competitions they use an MSA of about 14 to 18 degrees.
- From MSA, each of their feet during sweep moves backward about eight to 12 degrees (their ROS) before striking the ground with an SAT of approximately six degrees.
- Their collision with the ground is accomplished by means of a midfoot- to forefoot-strike.
- Their ROS/MSA ratio is close to .7.

With very few exceptions, these are the form characteristics which—when combined with superior metabolic capacities during exercise—allow a runner to enter the club of world-class distance runners.

Form Differences Between International and American Elite Runners

International runners dominate American harriers in elite distance competitions. It is tempting and logical to suggest that running form disparities play a key role in creating these performance differences.

For example, American elites are less likely to run with a midfoot-strike pattern and are more likely to run with a heel-strike, thus increasing the duration and magnitude of braking (and breaking) forces and amplifying the rate of increase of vertical ground-reaction forces with every step. Notable American examples of such running include Desiree (Desi) Linden (figure 13.1) and Shalane Flanagan (figure 13.2).

Compared with international elites, American elites also tend to have diminished ROS. This causes less kinetic energy to reach the ground per

Figure 13.1 Elite U.S. runner Desi Davila Linden has been a heel-striker throughout her career, with SATs as high as 16 degrees and ROS/MSA ratios as low as .27.

Figure 13.2 Elite U.S. runner Shalane Flanagan has also been a heel-striker throughout much of her career, with ROS/MSA ratios at .50 and below.

step, higher SATs (thus producing greater braking and breaking forces), and smaller ROS/MSA ratios (a reflection and cause of their generally slower running speeds in international competitions).

Elite U.S. female distance runners have highly unfavorable form characteristics, compared with their East-African competitors (table 13.1). Note that only one American runner (Jordan Hasay) has a "golden ratio" (ROS/MSA) greater than .5 on both legs. In fact, only one other American athlete (Molly Huddle) has a golden ratio above .5 on either leg. Also, notice that Molly Huddle is the only mid-foot striker with a negative FAT on each foot, while Jordan Hasay lands flat-footed. Amy Cragg is a slight heel-striker on her left foot (FAT = 1). Kara Goucher is a minimal heel striker on her right foot (FAT = 1), and otherwise all other contacts with the ground involve strong heel-striking with FAT at positive 6 and above (and as high as +20 for Kellyn Taylor). Given the disparities between right and left legs, the preference for heel-striking, and the very poor ROS/MSA ratios, it appears that elite U.S. female distance runners conduct very little form training.

The contrast in running-form metrics between the eight elite international women (including seven from East Africa) in table 13.2 and the elite

TABLE 13.1

Running Form Metrics: Elite American Women

NAME	EVENT	LEG	MSA	ROS	SAT	FAT	ROS/MSA RATIO
Molly Huddle	Track training	Right	23	9	14	−12	0.39
		Left	26	14	12	−9	0.54
Shalane Flanagan	2016 U.S. Olympic Marathon Trials	Right	17	8	9	13	0.47
		Left	14	7	7	6	0.50
Amy Cragg	2016 U.S. Olympic Marathon Trials	Right	17	7	10	7	0.41
		Left	15	7	8	1	0.47
Sara Hall	Road training	Right	19	5	14	10	0.26
		Left	16	2	14	9	0.13
Desiree Linden (Davila)	2011 Boston Marathon	Right	22	6	16	11	0.27
		Left	21	10	11	11	0.48
Jordan Hasay	10K Race	Right	18	12	6	0	0.67
		Left	16	10	6	0	0.60
Kellyn Taylor	Road training	Right	16	4	12	20	0.25
		Left	10	2	8	8	0.20
Kara Goucher	2011 Boston Marathon	Right	18	5	13	1	0.28
		Left	20	3	17	10	0.15

Courtesy of Walt Reynolds, NovaSport Athlete Development.

American women could not be more stark. Please note that the international women have a "golden ratio" (ROS/MSA) greater than .5 in all cases except one (Caroline Kilel). This indicates the American elites are creating greater braking forces per step—and experiencing longer durations of braking forces during each "visit" to the ground (stance). Note also in particular the relative consistency of SAT values for the international women, with most SAT being in the five- to eight-degree range. Paula Radcliffe is an exception here, but note her exceptionally large golden ratios. Gelete Burka has rather large values for SAT, but compensates with expansive values for ROS and thus has very good golden ratios. Please examine in particular the values for the incredibly explosive Almaz Ayana (2015 World Champion at 5000 Meters, 2016 Olympic Games Gold Medalist at 10,000 Meters (29:12), and 2017 World Champion at 10,000 Meters): Almaz has superb values of ROS/MSA on her right (.85) and left (.70) legs. Her incredible speed comes from these long, high-powered sweeps (ROS values) leading to explosive "punches" of the ground.

TABLE 13.2

Running Form Metrics: Elite International Women

NAME	EVENT	LEG	MSA	ROS	SAT	FAT	ROS/MSA RATIO
Mary Keitany	2010 NYC Marathon	Right	10	5	5	5	0.53
		Left	10	5	5	0	0.54
Tirunesh Dibaba	2013 Tilburg Netherlands 10K Road Race	Right	16	10	6	−2	0.63
		Left	20	12	8	−4	0.60
Almaz Ayana	2015 Weltklasse Zurich DL 3K	Right	20	17	3	−5	0.85
		Left	20	14	6	−6	0.70
Genzebe Dibaba	2015 Carlsbad 5K Road Race	Right	17	12	5	−12	0.71
		Left	25	18	7	−4	0.72
Caroline Kilel	2011 Boston Marathon	Right	16	7	9	−2	0.44
		Left	8	3	5	−3	0.38
Paula Radcliffe	2008 NYC Marathon	Right	8	7	1	−1	0.88
		Left	2	3	−1	−5	1.50
Gelete Burka	2015 IAAF 10K World Champs Track	Right	24	14	10	0	0.58
		Left	24	13	11	0	0.54
Aberu Kebede	2013 Tokyo Marathon	Right	8	5	3	−5	0.63
		Left	12	7	5	−3	0.58

Courtesy of Walt Reynolds, NovaSport Athlete Development.

The Non-Elite Runner

While there can be significant variations among runners, form characteristics for the ordinary runner share a number of common points.

ROS and MSA

MSA tends to be greater in the average distance runner, compared to the elite competitor. Conversely, the non-elite distance runner has very little ROS and tends to simply drop the foot to the ground after attaining MSA, instead of sweeping the foot backward dramatically to make contact with the ground. Because the ROS/MSA ratio is much smaller in the non-elite runner, it sometimes descends to a speed-thwarting 0.1, instead of the 0.7 used by the elite runner. The average runner you see jogging down the street in your neighborhood usually has an MSA of 18 and SAT of 16, putting the ROS/MSA ratio at a miserable 2/16, or .125, a proportion that maximizes slowing and braking and minimizes forward propulsive forces and kinetic energy transferred to the ground.

ROS and SAT

Since ROS tends to be greatly reduced in the non-elite distance runner, it produces an SAT that is significantly greater in the non-elite runner, possibly as high as 16 degrees (figure 13.3).

This is a key reason why the ordinary runner experiences considerably greater braking forces, compared with the elite harrier. This is also why the non-elite runner produces the high vertical ground-reaction forces at exactly the wrong time (while the shank angle is still positive and before the shank has reached a position perpendicular with the ground). It is as though the non-elite runner is trying to pole-vault forward using his leg as a pole, instead of bouncing forward explosively after ground contact.

Heel-Strike Pattern and Braking Forces

The ordinary runner tends to land with a less-flexed knee and a straighter leg at touchdown, which augments the rate of transmission of braking forces through the leg, increases braking forces, and decreases the ability of the knee joint to act as a shock absorber and force dissipater after impact with the ground. In addition, the non-elite runner is much more likely to land on the ground with a heel-strike pattern. In fact, research reveals that up to 95 percent of all non-elite distance runners collide with the ground in this way (2).

Figure 13.3 The "runner on the street" is a very poor "sweeper", reversing swing by just two degrees and hitting the ground with an SAT of ~16.

Time on the Ground

The average runner spends much more time on the ground per step, compared with the elite competitor. In fact, research reveals that ordinary distance runners may spend as much as 70 percent of their total running time on the ground during gait, versus less than 50 percent for elite runners. More time stuck on the ground means less time flying forward and therefore slower running speeds for non-elites. When running at 10-K race velocity, the elite runner may spend approximately 160 to 180 milliseconds on the ground per step, versus about 220 milliseconds for the common runner.

The Distance Runner Versus the Sprinter

High-quality sprinters share a few form characteristics with high-performance distance runners. For example, SAT tends to be quite similar—averaging about six to eight degrees—in both top sprinters and distance runners. ROS/MSA ratios also tend to be similar between the two groups, hovering near .7. For example, Usain Bolt (figure 13.4a), the world's fastest man with a 100-meter world record time of 9:58, and Eliud Kipchoge (figure 13.4b), the worlds' fastest marathon runner with a non-world-record time of 2:00:24, both have golden ratios (ROS/MSA) of .7.

However, there are also some key differences between sprinters and distance runners. For example, MSA is much greater in the elite sprinter,

Figure 13.4 (a) World's-best sprinter Usain Bolt and (b) world's-best marathon runner Eliud Kipchoge share the same golden ratio.

compared with the elite distance harrier (it is often twice as large). This is a reflection of the higher speeds obtained by the elite sprinter, which require that the "hammer" (leg) of the "pistol" (body) be cocked to a greater degree so that it can accelerate toward the ground for a longer period. This allows the leg to attain a higher velocity in the instant before ground contact, thus putting more kinetic energy into the ground. World-record holder Usain Bolt often attains an MSA of 28 degrees when he competes at 100 meters, whereas marathon world-record holder Dennis Kimetto ordinarily uses an MSA of around 14 degrees per step when he competes in the marathon (and Eliud Kipchoge used only 10 degrees when he ran his amazing 2:00:24). During competition, Kimetto does not run as fast as Bolt, so he can set his leg about half as far ahead of his body, compared with Usain. While Kipchoge does not cock his leg as far ahead as Kimetto, he has a better ROS, helping to account for his faster marathon pace.

Since SAT is similar between elite sprinters and elite distance runners, it seems obvious that ROS must be strikingly different. Bolt, for example, sweeps back from 28 degrees to about eight degrees of positive SAT (an ROS of 20 degrees); Kimetto starts at 14 degrees and comes back to six or seven degrees (an ROS of seven to eight degrees). Thus ROS/MSA is 20/28 = .71 for Bolt (figure 13.5) and 8/14 = .57 for Kimetto (figure 13.6).

ALEXANDER NEMENOV/AFP/Getty Images

Figure 13.5 **Bolt has an MSA of around 28 and an SAT of about 7.**

AFP/Getty Images

Figure 13.6 **Dennis Kimetto (at far left) has an MSA of around 14 and an SAT of 6 to 7.**

As mentioned, these form disparities help to produce the large differences in performance velocity between Bolt and Kimetto. Bolt's more-expansive ROS imparts greater kinetic energy to the ground per step, compared with Kimetto's less-bold reversal of foot movement. In addition, Bolt's leg is moving much more quickly than Kimetto's leg during ROS: Research suggests that Bolt's leg may be clocking backward at about 300 to 350 degrees per second during ROS, while Kimetto's leg moves at closer to 100 to 150 degrees per second (3).

The angular velocity of the shank during ground contact is also dramatically different between sprinters and distance runners, with sprinters reaching more than 1,000 degrees per second and elite distance runners reaching about 500 degrees per second. Non-elites will have slower angular velocities during stance, but the differences between sprinters and distance runners will still be present.

Ground-contact time (stance) is also quite different between elite sprinters and elite distance runners. Usain Bolt stays on the ground for no longer than 83 milliseconds per step when competing at 100 meters, while other notable sprinters such as Carl Lewis and Justin Gatlin have had their ground-contact times measured at between 83 and 100 milliseconds. By contrast, elite distance runners tend to be stuck on the ground for about 160 milliseconds per contact, and the ordinary runner remains lodged against the earth for a considerably longer 220 milliseconds or more per step.

The Sprinter's "Air" Leg

Up to this point, this chapter has focused almost entirely on the "ground" leg—the lower leg that is immediately poised for contact with the ground or is actually on the ground. However, when it comes to measurements and comments about form, it is also important to mention the "air" leg—the leg that has just left the ground and is moving backward and then forward prior to reaching MSA, thus tracing the back and upper margins of the kidney bean path mentioned in chapter 1. Naturally, during running an air leg is always about to become a ground leg, and a ground leg is on the verge of becoming the air leg as a runner moves forward. The right and left legs repeatedly change roles during gait.

In sprinting, the air leg plays a particularly prominent role. The idea in sprinting is to maximize vertical ground reaction force when each foot is on the ground, and the air leg assists the ground leg in this task.

To understand this, weigh yourself on a bathroom scale. As you look down at the number, notice that your weight actually changes slightly as you move around during scale stance, even with subtle shifts in foot pressure and body position. Now swing your arms overhead while watching the scale reading. What happens? It is likely the swing of the arms upward instantly increased your "weight" by causing more force to be applied to the surface of the scale. This is the inevitable acting out of one of Newton's original laws of motion: For every action, there is an equal and opposite reaction. The upward thrusting of your arms (resulting from a force directed overhead) created an equal and opposite reaction, with a force directed down into the scale.

This means that in running, an upward thrust of the air leg (the so-called "high-knee" action) amplifies the force placed on the earth by the ground leg, increasing vertical propulsive force. This is why (at initial ground contact) the air leg of the sprinter is always further advanced through swing, compared with the air leg of the distance runner (figures 13.7 and 13.8). The air leg of the sprinter must be poised to drive upward at the moment of first contact with the earth by the ground leg, in order to maximize vertical ground reaction force. The air leg is helping the ground leg push into the running surface and thus is increasing velocity.

This reinforces the notion that sprinters should attempt to minimize "backside mechanics" during their training—that is, they should train in

Figure 13.7   The sprinter's "air thigh" must be higher during mid-stance of the ground leg, compared with the distance-runner's air thigh, in order to increase the magnitude of propulsive force produced by the ground leg.

Figure 13.8   The distance runner's "air thigh" must be lower during mid-stance of the ground leg, compared with the sprinter's air thigh, because of the lower magnitudes of propulsive force required in the ground leg.

ways that increase the speed of movement of the leg after toe-off so that the swing leg can be in a position to drive upward as the other (ground) leg makes contact with earth.

Male Versus Female Runners

Popular articles often suggest that running form is somehow different in women compared with men, and they often place the focus on the angle made between the thigh and hip joint. This "Q angle" is often larger in women because of their generally wider hips in relation to their body size (figure 13.9). The implications of this difference are never made entirely clear, but one possibility is that women might tend to land on the ground with a slightly more supinated ankle, which then might cause them to go through a greater range of pronation during stance and perhaps spike the rate of injury. In other words, women might be more likely to land on the outsides (lateral edges) of their shoes compared with men, which would then lead to a greater inward roll-ing of the ankle (pronation) during stance.

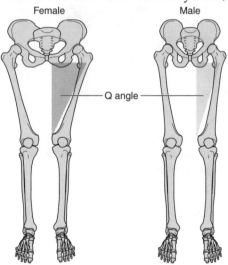

Figure 13.9 **The greater Q angle of female runners might increase the risks of ankle-supinated landings, greater pronation during stance, and thus injury.**

However, new research indicates the pronation is not actually linked with a higher rate of injury (4). Fur-thermore, the laws of physics do not vary according to the gender of a runner. The form variables discussed in this book—foot-strike pattern, MSA, ROS, SAT, and ROS/MSA ratio—are optimized in the same way in male and female runners since the movements of their bodies are both sub-ject to Newton's Laws of Motion. A study of male and female world-record holders shows that the basic form metrics are identical for men and women at distances ranging from 200 meters up to the marathon (3). (There is one world-record-holding outlier—Florence Griffith Joyner—who, as she set the world record for 100 meters, had an unusually large MSA of around 34 degrees and an SAT of about 12 degrees.) This means that the overall process of training and optimizing the relevant form variables will be the same in male and female runners.

That being said, one might make the logical argument that form training could still be more important from an injury prevention standpoint for female runners. With the Q angle being greater in women, there is greater torque created at the hip compared with men, and thus foot-strike pattern would be especially critical. A heel-strike pattern would create dramatically greater torque forces at the hip in a shorter period of time, compared with a midfoot- strike, which is associated with a smaller VALR.

Older Versus Younger Runners

As is the case with the male-female contrast, masters and open runners experience the same forces during running and need to optimize the same form metrics. Form training will thus be very similar in runners, regardless of age.

That being said, masters runners tend to have more problems with backside mechanics, compared with younger runners. After toe-off, masters runners tend to have less hip extension compared with younger runners, and the movement of the swinging leg when it is behind the body tends to be more lethargic in older runners. Because the leg tends to move more slowly, it is prone to be late moving into proper position for the time-sensitive upward knee thrust of the air leg.

This can be corrected by training, using the drills in chapters 8 and 14. The lack of hip extension in masters runners is also a function of not only what happens during rearward-directed swing of the leg after toe-off, but also of a slower angular velocity of the ground leg during stance. Since the leg is generally moving more slowly during stance in the masters runner, the velocity of the foot at take-off is lower and thus hip extension is reduced. This situation can at least be partially rectified through the use of running-specific strengthening exercises, drills that emphasize minimization of ground-contact time, and dynamic mobility work to increase the flexibility of the hip flexors (which resist hip extension).

The Right-Leg Versus Left-Leg Runner

Not only is there considerable variation among all runners when it comes to form characteristics and metrics, but there is also significant variation within an individual runner. That is, the action of a runner's left or right leg may vary a bit from one encounter with the ground to the next. However, all runners have a distinct, signature pattern with each leg. The behavior of the right or left leg tends to converge around basic values of the form variables.

The biggest variation that occurs in an individual runner is from the right leg to the left leg. Somewhat surprisingly, the majority of runners have legs that function differently, with the right leg having different metrics (MSA, SAT, ROS, ROS/MSA, and even foot-strike pattern) compared with the left.

These disparities can be strikingly large. For example, my own work with an elite runner has revealed that, during competition, her left leg has an MSA of 18 degrees, an SAT of 6 degrees, an ROS of 12, an ROS/MSA ratio of 12/18 = .67, and a beautiful midfoot-strike pattern. On the right leg, however, the MSA is 17 degrees, the SAT is 10 degrees, the ROS is 7, the ROS/MSA ratio is only 7/17 = .41, and the foot-strike pattern is a disturbing heel-strike. Despite these large differences, this elite runner was unaware of the disparate behavior exhibited by her lower limbs. This disparity was fully corrected utilizing the drills outlined in this book.

This situation is actually a dream scenario for coaches. For the first time, we have real metrics regarding form and thus something specific we can really aim for as we coach our athletes. It is exciting to know that we can improve the speed and stamina of our athletes not only through long periods of challenging training, but also through the process of form optimization, which can take considerably less time to achieve. Form work is really the foundation of all running training and should be engaged in seriously from the outset of training. Otherwise, a runner may end up with one "victorious" leg and one "defeating" leg—or with generally poor form that negates all of the metabolic advances she makes through arduous training. With poor form, even a runner who has the strongest heart and muscles with the highest oxidative capacities will be, in effect, running with a Rolls-Royce engine and square wheels. Fortunately, we as coaches now have real numbers (for MSA, ROS, SAT, ROS/MSA, and FAT) that we can use as goals and guides as we teach optimal form to our runners.

Summary

When it comes to improving form, the task for every runner (male, female, sprinter, distance runner, young, and old) is the same: He or she must learn how to coordinate repetitive collisions with the ground in a way that optimizes MSA, SAT, ROS, ROS/MSA, and FAT. Doing so will simultaneously increase running speed and endurance while decreasing the risk of injury.

There are huge differences in these variables between the average runner and the elite distance runner, but the average runner should attempt to move his form numbers toward those achieved by the best elites. In doing so, he might not set a world record, but his performances will improve, and his risk of injury will decrease.

Sprinting and distance running do have striking form differences, with sprinters relying on forefoot-strikes, while distance runners who are interested in optimizing form go for midfoot-striking. Sprinters also exhibit greater MSA, an ROS that is greater in magnitude, higher angular velocity during ROS, greater angular velocity during ground sweep, shorter stance durations, and higher cadences.

References

1. Walter Reynolds, "Maximal Shank Angle, Reversal of Swing, and Shank Angle at Touchdown in World-Record Elite Distance Performances," unpublished (2015).
2. H. Hasegawa et al., "Foot-Strike Patterns at the 15-km Point During an Elite-Level Half Marathon," *Journal of Strength and Conditioning Research* 21, no. 3 (2007): 888–893.
3. Walt Reynolds, personal communication, February 7, 2017.
4. B.M. Nigg et al., "Running Shoes and Running Injuries: Mythbusting and a Proposal for Two New Paradigms: 'Preferred Movement Path' and 'Comfort Filter,'" *British Journal of Sports Medicine* 49, no. 20 (2015): 1290–1294.

14

Running-Specific Strength Training

Running-specific strength training enhances six variables that are critical for running performance:

1. The amount of vertical force applied to the ground per step
2. The amount of horizontal propulsive force applied to the ground per step
3. The angular velocity of the shank during ground contact
4. The time required per step to apply vertical and horizontal propulsive forces and thus cadence
5. The amount of vertical propulsive force added to the ground-contact leg by the swing leg
6. Maximal vertical propulsive force (the key predictor of max running velocity)

It is essential to make strength training specific to running. Running-specific strength training mimics the mechanics of gait. Thus, the gains in strength that are attained translate directly and specifically into the movements of running.

In chapter 8, the Explosive Workout Routines emphasized applying propulsive force to the ground more quickly. The workout in this chapter focuses on increasing running-specific strength—specifically on applying more propulsive force to the ground during stance.

Previous chapters have explained the importance of the trajectory of the foot during gait in establishing proper form. The foot should travel in a pattern shaped like a kidney bean, with the front of the bean shaped like the point of a spear (figure 14.1*a*).

The spear point is itself extraordinary because it represents the fact that the foot and shin reach an optimal forward point and then are actively and dramatically brought back to the ground at high speed. This enhances ROS and the all-important ROS/MSA ratio, which provides an instant report card on a runner's form.

Unfortunately, the average runner displays nothing resembling a spear point during gait. Runners more typically move the foot and shin forward and then (after reaching MSA), let the foot fall tragically to earth, with little ROS, a small amount of kinetic energy applied to the ground, and an injury-promoting heel-strike (figure 14.1*b* and *c*). Running-specific strength

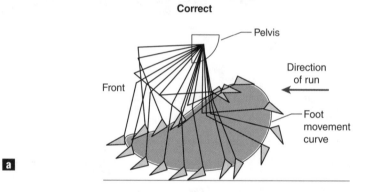

Figure 14.1 (*a*) During running, the pattern of foot movement creates a kidney bean shape with—optimally—a "spear point" at the front of the bean. (*b*) The runner with great form swings the foot well ahead of the body, but then (*c*) she brings it most of the way back to the body before letting it strike the ground, creating a "spear point" to the kidney bean.

training can correct such flaws by improving control of the foot and ankle during swing, spiking the magnitude and velocity of ROS, and magnifying the quantity of kinetic energy imparted to the ground.

Workout to Improve Running-Specific Strength

When performing the running-specific, strength-promoting exercises in this chapter, try to maintain a feeling that you are actually running. Don't tense your upper body and gaze downward at your legs as you exercise; you wouldn't do that while running. Also, perform the exercises rhythmically and smoothly, not with choppy timing and movements. After an adequate warm-up, carry out the following exercises.

1. ONE-LEG SQUATS

This exercise enhances vertical propulsive force during ground contact, promotes stability during stance, and upgrades running economy and fatigue resistance.

Repetition

Perform two sets of 12 reps on each leg, with a short break of about 10 seconds in between.

Action

Maintain good posture as you squat. Don't lean forward with your upper body, rather let your torso descend during the squat until the hip of the squatting (support) leg is on a level with the knee. Then, straighten the leg and return to starting position. Balance the toes of the rear foot on a step or bench behind you, being careful not to bear any weight on the rear foot. During each squat, the knee of the non-support, rear leg should descend downward toward a line perpendicular to the support foot at the heel. Begin the one-leg squats with no added resistance. As strength and stability increase, gradually add resistance by holding steadily heavier dumbbells or by positioning a weighty bar on the shoulders (figure 14.2a and b).

Figure 14.2 (*a*) Starting position for the one-leg squat. (*b*) "Down" position for the one-leg squat.

2. RUNNER'S POSES

This exercise enhances the ability of the swing leg to assist the ground-contact leg in applying vertical propulsive force to the ground.

Repetition

Perform two sets of 15 poses per leg.

Action

To carry out this exercise, stand relaxed and straight, with your feet placed on either side of an imaginary midline running down through your body. Then, swing your right thigh ahead and upward until it is just above a position which would be parallel with the floor. Your right leg should flex at the knee as you do this, so that the lower part of the leg points almost directly at the ground, nearly perpendicular. Your left foot should support your full body weight. As you swing your right thigh ahead and upward, simultaneously bring your left arm forward, as you would during a normal running stride. In your support (left) leg, the hip, knee, and ankle should all be slightly flexed. Hold this position—with the right leg up—for a few seconds, while maintaining relaxed stability and balance. Then, bring your right foot back to the ground and your left arm back to a relaxed position at your side, thus completing one pose or repetition.

Perform 14 more reps with your right thigh swinging upward, and then switch over to your left leg for 15 poses. Your right leg should now support your entire body weight. Repeat, with one more set on each leg. As you become stronger and more skilled and coordinated, increase the speed of the thigh-lift move, and then resist it with the use of a medium- to high-resistance stretch cord (figure 14.3*a* and *b*).

Figure 14.3   (*a*) Basic position for Runner's Poses. (*b*) Thigh-up position for Runner's Poses.

3. TOE-WALKING WITH OPPOSITE-ANKLE DORSIFLEXION

This exercise improves the strength of the "arch" and plantar structures of the foot, fostering more productive midfoot-strikes. It also augments the dynamic strength and mobility of the Achilles tendon and calf muscles, allowing the runner to carry out midfoot-strikes in a more controlled, stable, and energy-returning manner—with less risk of injury.

Repetition

Perform two sets of 20 meters, with a 10-second break between sets.

Action

Stand as tall as you can on your toes. Balance for a moment, and then begin walking forward on your toes with slow, small steps. Take one step every one to two seconds, with each step being about 10 to 12 inches (25 to 30 centimeters) in length. As you do this, maintain a tall, balanced posture. Dorsi-flex the ankle and toes of the free, forward-moving leg upward as high as possible with each step—moving the toes of the swing foot as close to the shin as possible—while maintaining your balance on the toes and ball of the support foot (figure 14.4a and b).

Figure 14.4 (*a*) Stay high on the toes while carrying out this exercise. (*b*) Be sure to dorsi-flex the swing ankle as it moves forward.

4. LUNGES WITH BALANCE-CHALLENGING AND CORE-BUILDING BALL MOVEMENT

This exercise is great for leg strength, core strength, upper-body strength, and balance. It also helps runners build their core strength in a running-specific way and thus makes their upper bodies more stable during running. The result is better overall form and improved economy. Make progress with this exercise by gradually increasing the number of repetitions and the weight of the medicine ball.

Repetition

Perform two sets of 10 reps per leg.

Action

Stand in a running-ready position, with your feet pointed straight ahead and shoulder-width apart. Your ankles, knees, and hips should be very lightly flexed. The abs and buttocks should be slightly tightened, pulling the bottom of your pelvis forward. Shoulders should be relaxed and in a "down" position, not held up and forward. Hold a medicine ball that weighs about seven to 11 pounds (three to five kilograms) in your hands, depending on your strength. Take a long step forward with your left foot, landing in the midfoot area, and quickly yet smoothly move into a lunge squat so that your left thigh is parallel with the ground. As you do this, your right foot will rock up onto its toes. Preserve this position, and use your right foot only for balance, not for bearing weight. Hold the medicine ball on the outside of your left knee (figure 14.5a), and then with a very smooth action lift the medicine ball up, forward, and to the right, so that the ball ends up high above your right shoulder (and actually a little to the right) (figure 14.5b). Hold your trunk upright, and keep your arms relatively straight as you perform this movement; don't allow the arms to flex at the elbows. This diagonal swing upward strengthens the core and upper body and is also destabilizing to the lunge position (thus enhancing leg strength and stability). Try to preserve a perfect lunge position and the stability of your trunk as you carry out the movement. Once the medicine ball has reached its highest point, return it quickly yet smoothly to the outside of your left knee (in a chopping motion) to complete one rep.

Complete 10 total reps in this way, and then change the lunge position. This time lunge forward with your right foot. Hold the lunge stance with the right foot as the support foot and the back, left foot serving as the balance structure. Otherwise repeat the basic movements of the exercise for 10 repetitions. This time the ball will be held outside the right knee and will be thrust forward, up above the left shoulder, and slightly to the left before being returned to the outside of the right knee with a chopping motion.

Figure 14.5   (*a*) Starting point for Lunges With Balance-Challenging and Core-Building Ball Movement, with the ball held just lateral to the support knee. (*b*) Midway position for Lunges with Balance-Challenging and Core-Building Ball Movement, with the ball held with straight arms high above the shoulder opposite the support (lunging) leg.

5. BALANCE AND ECCENTRIC REACHES WITH TOES

This exercise enhances stability of the foot, ankle, and leg during ground contact and thus permits an increased angular velocity of the shank during stance as well as the production of greater vertical propulsive force. In addition, this activity enhances the strength of the Achilles tendon and calf complex and thus decreases the risk of injury when running with a midfoot-strike pattern.

Repetition

Perform three sets of 10 reps (that is, 10 straight ahead, 10 lateral, and 10 medial reps) with each foot.

Action

To carry out this exercise correctly, start by standing on your right foot as you face a wall or other structure, with the toes of your right foot about 30 to 36 inches (.7 to .9 meters) from the wall (you may need to adjust this distance slightly as you perform the exercise). Your left foot should be off the ground and positioned toward the front of your body, with the left leg relatively straight. Then, bend your right leg at the knee while maintaining your upper body posture in a relatively vertical position, nearly directly over your right foot. As you bend your right leg in a squatting movement, move your left foot toward the wall until your toes actually touch the wall, keeping your left leg relatively straight (figure 14.6a). End the movement by returning to the starting position. Repeat this action—squatting on the right leg while reaching forward to the wall with the left foot—10 times.

Next, conduct essentially the same activity, but this time move your left foot forward and to the left (diagonally and laterally), keeping your left leg straight as you attempt to make contact with the wall (figure 14.6b). As you do this, control your right, weight-bearing foot so that it does not roll sharply to the inside. Note that your left foot may not quite reach the wall, since you are moving in a frontal plane (from right to left) in addition to the straight-ahead, sagittal plane (from back to front). Make sure that you are completing a nice squat on your right leg as you reach with your left foot. As you complete this squat and reach, you should feel strong tension and a twisting action in your right Achilles tendon (actions which will ultimately enhance the strength and injury resistance of your Achilles). Repeat this movement (diagonal to the left) 10 times.

After the final rep, return to the starting position. Then carry out essentially the same activity, but with your left foot crossing over the front of your body medially and moving to the right as you attempt to touch the wall (figure 14.6c). As you do this, control your right foot and right ankle so that the right foot does not roll significantly to its outside edge. When you return to the starting position, you have completed one medial rep on your right foot. Complete 10 medial reps in all.

Throughout this entire exercise, keep your upper body straight and relaxed. Don't lean backward or to one side or the other with your torso. You should continue standing tall, facing the wall, as you do each rep in all three versions (straight, lateral, and medial). Make sure that your support foot is also pointing directly toward the wall. Once you have completed a full set (10 straight ahead, 10 lateral, and 10 medial) on the right foot, complete a full set with your left foot as the weight-bearing foot and the right foot as the trotter that is moving toward the wall (first straight ahead for 10 reps, then laterally for 10 reps, and then medially for 10 reps).

Figure 14.6   (*a*) Balance and eccentric reaches with toes with each reach taking place straight ahead. (*b*) Balance and eccentric reaches with toes using a lateral reach. (*c*) Balance and eccentric reaches with toes using a medial reach.

6. HIGH BENCH STEP-UPS

This exercise enhances stability during ground contact and improves vertical propulsive force.

Repetition

Perform two sets of 10 reps on each leg.

Action

Begin in a standing position on top of a high bench or step—about six to eight inches (15 to 20 centimeters) high—with your body weight on your right foot. Your left foot should be free and held slightly behind your body. Using a squatting action with your right leg, lower your body in a controlled manner until the toes of your left foot touch the ground behind the bench, but continue to support all of your weight on your right foot (figure 14.7a). Then, push downward on the bench with your right foot and straighten your right leg (figure 14.7b). As you do this, swing your left leg upward and forward until your left thigh is parallel with the surface of the bench (similar to the stance you adopted when doing the "Runner's Poses" earlier in this workout). As your left thigh swings upward, your left leg should be bent at the knee, and your right arm should swing forward naturally as your left leg swings up and ahead. Hold this position, with the left leg up for a moment; this completes one rep. Then slowly and smoothly squat with your right leg, and lower your left toes to the ground behind the bench, beginning your second repetition.

Continue in this manner for the prescribed number of reps, and then switch over so that your body weight is supported on your left leg as you complete the required reps. Maintain upright posture with your trunk throughout the entire exercise. Sustain good control of your body as you squat and lower one foot behind the bench—do not lean forward with your torso. The foot that is being lowered behind the bench should lightly touch the ground behind the bench; it is not used for weight-bearing at all. The foot is lowered not by reaching for the ground, but by squatting with the other, weight-bearing leg.

Make progress with this exercise by increasing the number of repetitions, by holding dumbbells in the hands, and by gradually increasing the weight of the dumbbells.

Figure 14.7 (*a*) "Down" position for bench step-ups, with the non-support toes just touching the floor behind the bench. (*b*) "Up" position for the bench step-ups, with the non-support thigh brought up.

7. BICYCLE LEG SWINGS WITH STRETCH BAND

This activity is great for improving control of the foot and shin during forward swing, promoting better ROS after MSA is reached, and upgrading the functional strength and fatigue resistance of the hamstrings.

Repetition

Perform two sets of 50 reps per leg.

Action

To perform these swings, stand with your weight fully supported on your left leg. Initially, you may place your right hand on a wall or other support to maintain balance. Begin by flexing your right hip and raising your right knee to waist height so that your right thigh is parallel with the ground (figure 14.8a). As you do this, your right knee should be flexed to 90 degrees or more. Once your thigh is parallel to the ground, begin to extend your right knee (swing the lower part of your right leg forward, with an un-flexed knee) until your knee is nearly fully extended and your leg is nearly straight. The right thigh should still be parallel to the ground. After your right knee nears full extension, allow your right thigh to drop downward and backward (figure 14.8b). Then begin flexing your right knee, "paw" or scrape the ground under your body with the right foot, and continue until the entire thigh and leg are extended behind your body (as if you were following through on a running stride) (figure 14.8c). As your right hip nears full extension and you approach the end of the backswing, raise your right heel by bending your right knee. Your right heel should move closely towards your buttocks as you do this. As this happens, begin moving your right knee forward until it returns to the appropriate position in front of your body, with your right thigh parallel to the ground. Repeat this entire sequence of actions in a smooth and continuous manner.

Once you are able to coordinate the overall movements, strive to perform the swings at a cadence of about 12 swings every 10 seconds or so. When you have achieved full coordination of the basic actions, attach a strong stretch cord to your swing (non-support) ankle at one end. Attach the other end of the stretch cord to a firm post, table leg, fence, railing, or other structure (at roughly knee height). Stand facing the post with enough distance between you and the structure so that the stretch cord significantly accelerates your leg forward during the forward swing. This enhanced forward acceleration will put your hamstrings under stress, which will ultimately strengthen your hamstrings.

Make progress with this exercise by increasing the number of repetitions and by using steadily heavier stretch cords. You will know that you are performing the exercise correctly if you experience significant fatigue in the hamstrings as you complete the movements.

Figure 14.8   (*a*) During Bicycle Leg Swings, the stretch cord pulls the non-support leg forward rapidly during swing. (*b*) At the end of ROS, the non-support foot "paws" the ground aggressively. (*c*) At the end of hip extension and back swing, the non-support leg is poised to move forward again.

8. REVERSE BICYCLE LEG SWINGS WITH STRETCH BAND

This exercise enhances MSA and the ability of the swing leg to augment the vertical propulsive force produced by the ground-contact leg. That is because it swings upward and forward more aggressively while off the ground which, per Newton's Law, increases the downward force applied by the support leg to the ground.

Repetition

Perform two sets of 50 reps per leg.

Action

This exercise is exactly like the Regular Bicycle Leg Swings prescribed previously, except that you are facing away from the post where the stretch cord is attached. The cord then resists forward leg swing, instead of enhancing it. Make progress by gradually increasing the number of repetitions and the resistance of the stretch cord (figures 14.9*a* and *b*).

Figure 14.9 (*a*) This time, the forward swing of the leg is resisted—not aided—by the stretch cord, thus building tremendous hip-flexion strength. (*b*) The cord actually pulls the leg back for full hip extension prior to the next forward swing.

9. PARTIAL SQUATS

This exercise enhances stability during ground contact and also augments maximum vertical propulsive force.

Repetition

Perform one set on each leg.

Action

Stand with your right foot directly under your right shoulder, keeping your right knee just slightly flexed and maintaining a relaxed, upright posture. If desired, hold light dumbbells in your hands. Incline your whole body forward just slightly from the right ankle. Your body weight should be directed through the midfoot of the right foot. Your left leg should be flexed at the knee so that the left foot is not touching the ground at all (figure 14.10a). The left foot should be suspended in air—however, as you carry out partial squats you may occasionally need to briefly touch the floor with your trailing leg for balance as you complete this exercise.

If you were carrying out a traditional one-leg squat, you would bend your right leg at the knee at this point and lower your body until the right knee reached an angle of about 90 degrees between the back of your thigh and lower leg. At this point, your thigh would be almost parallel with the ground. However, for this partial squat, simply descend about halfway to the ground so that the angle between the back of your thigh and lower leg is roughly 135 degrees (figure 14.10b). Then, return to the starting position (with a nearly straight right leg), maintaining upright posture with your trunk.

Continue in the manner described above until you have completed 10 partial squats. Then, without resting, descend into the 11th partial squat but, instead of immediately rising upward, hold the partial-squat position (the 135-degree position) for 10 seconds. This is a static hold position.

After holding this static position for 10 seconds, immediately (without resting) perform 10 more partial squats, maintain another static hold for 10 seconds, perform 10 more reps, and then maintain another static hold for 10 seconds. This completes one set.

To summarize, a set proceeds as follows (with no recovery during the set):

1. 10 partial squats
2. 10 seconds of holding your leg and body in a static down position
3. 10 partial squats
4. 10 seconds in a static hold
5. 10 partial squats
6. 10 seconds in a static hold

Once this set is complete, carry out a similar set on your right leg. If you can complete a full set on each leg without having to stop, you may then increase the weight of the dumbbells. About 2.5 pounds (one kilogram) per dumbbell can incrementally increase the weight. Each time you are able to complete one set per leg without major problems, you may continue to add weight for subsequent workouts.

Figure 14.10   (*a*) Beginning position for the partial squat. (*b*) Down position for the partial squat.

Carry out this complete strength training workout to improve running-specific strength approximately twice per week during the strength-building phase of your training. Then conduct the Explosive Workout routine from chapter 8 about two times per week during the speed-building phase of your overall program. See chapter 15 to understand how to integrate form drills, running-specific strength training, and explosive training into your overall program.

Summary

Running-specific strength training has a profound effect on key running-form variables. Running-specific strength training can increase swing and thus maximum shank angle (MSA), the breadth and velocity of reversal of swing (ROS, or sweep), the amount of vertical force applied to the ground during stance, the amount of horizontal force applied to the ground during stance, the angular velocity of the shank during ground contact, the time required to apply optimal vertical and horizontal force to the ground during stance, and the amount of vertical propulsive force added to the ground-contact leg by the swing leg. Running-specific strength training also increases maximal vertical propulsive force, the key predictor of maximal running speed.

Thus running-specific strength training provides a great number and variety of benefits for running form, performance, and injury prevention and should be a fundamental foundation of the overall training program.

Integrating Form Work Into Your Seasonal Training

Just as we take a ground-up approach to the development of good running form—approaching it from the standpoint of controlling the way the foot and leg interact with the running surface rather than from the traditional approaches of making adjustments with the trunk, arms, shoulders, neck, and head—we must take a bottom-up approach to coordinating form work with the rest of training in an overall program. In other words, form work is the foundation of a runner's training program, not a collection of drills and exercises that should be sprinkled into the schedule here and there from week to week.

In fact, form work should precede all other forms of running training. The reasons for this are clear. First, poor running form increases the risk of injury by magnifying the ground-reaction forces that are experienced by a runner's legs and body. Embarking on a running program without a prior period of form training increases the risk that the development of fitness will be thwarted by workout-stopping injury.

Second, poor running form hurts running economy, heightens braking forces during contact with the ground, and slows running speed. As a result, it lowers overall training quality and slows the development of fitness over time. Starting a running program without a solid base of form training is like trying to sail around the world without a compass and map—and with a hole in the hull of the boat.

Form Work = Base Training

Form work is the new "base training" in a runner's overall approach to gaining fitness. Traditionally, base training has been defined as the earliest stage of a runner's overall training program, when he focused on running at moderate intensities while gradually increasing the number of miles (kilometers) completed during training. The basic underlying principle in traditional base training was that the unhurried increase in volume and intensity would prevent injuries from occurring and would permit a gradual and sustainable rise in running fitness.

A key flaw in this thinking is the notion that adherence to a moderate running pace will prevent injury. Scientific research indicates that the number of impacts with the ground—not speed of training—is the dominant cause of injury. Running slowly per se does not cut into the injury threat, especially if a traditional base period of moderate running is not preceded by form training and strengthening (1).

I wrote an advancement of the base-training concept in the book *Running Science* (2). In this new thinking, there was a call for an emphasis on strength training during the base period, particularly running-specific strength training (mimicking the mechanics of gait). This call came from the logical belief that such strength training would protect runners from the accumulated impact forces associated with striking the ground 180 times per minute with their feet.

However, as we have seen earlier in this book, the adoption of bad form increases the amount of shock force transmitted through the leg per step and also increases the rate at which that shock travels upward through the foot, ankle, leg, hips, and spine. While strength training can protect the body to some degree from such major upswings in ground-reaction force, a first-line form of protection involves creating a better "moment of truth," or a superior interaction of body with ground at the instant of impact that limits injury producing forces. This upgraded moment of truth features a midfoot-strike, rather than a bone-pummeling rear foot-crash. It also calls for a flexed knee and shank angle of around six to eight degrees at impact, rather than a straight leg (nonflexed knee) and a pathetic shank angle at impact (SAT) of 14 to 18 degrees (which in fact is the shank angle at impact adopted by the vast majority of runners).

Such an improved moment of truth can be developed readily with the use of the form drills outlined in this book. A superior way of interacting with the ground should be established before a runner embarks on any serious training, not as an afterthought as training pushes ahead recklessly.

The Change-Over From Bad to Good Form

Putting form first can be a tricky proposition for runners and coaches, as some runners establish good form within a few minutes while others may require a month or more to upgrade form significantly. For novice runners, it is important to remember that form should be learned first, before a training program expands in volume and intensity. For experienced runners with previously bad form, the amount of running carried out with good form should be gradually increased over time.

For example, a runner who has been running 30 miles (or 48 kilometers) per week or more with heel-strikes and high SATs will be in great peril of injury if she totally converts to midfoot-striking with an SAT of six to eight degrees—and then continues running 30 miles per week, with all the miles completed with great form. The magnitude and timing of the forces experienced by the bones, connective tissues, and muscles of the leg change strikingly when a runner changes form. Thus dramatic form makeovers can spell trouble when training load is relatively high, even when a runner is changing from poor to perfect form. A calf muscle fiber has no way of acknowledging a runner's great shift from bad to great form; it simply feels and reacts to the forces placed on it per step, which of course are greater during midfoot-striking, compared with heel-strikes.

This is all the more reason why form changes should occur before training volume expands from a low level. If a runner changes completely from heel-striking and high SATs to midfoot-striking and low SATs when she is running 10 miles (or 16 kilometers) per week of training, then the total, temporary strains on muscles and connective tissues will be far lower, compared with trying to make a sudden and complete overhaul at 50 miles (or 80 kilometers) per week. The runner with the greater mileage who changes from bad to good form can either drop down to a very low volume level once the good form is adopted or deliberately mix good-form and bad-form running over the course of each training week. Eventually the good form should occupy more and more of the overall training time.

Thus the modern concept of base training calls for a period of intensive form training, combined with strength training, which should be completed before a runner begins to make significant increases in training intensity and volume. The form training will consist of the drills and form sessions outlined in chapters 6 through 10. A coach should always bear in mind that letting one of her runners embark on mileage expansion without first being cured of heel-striking and large SATs represents irresponsible conduct and puts the runner at great risk of training-thwarting injury.

Table 15.1 is an example of an outstanding, four-week, form-building base period, with proper progressions in the form work (thanks to Walt Reynolds, CSCS, for providing this program).

TABLE 15.1

Run Form Drill Progression—Phase 1

DAY	INTRODUCTION - WEEK 1	WEEK 2	WEEK 3	WEEK 4
Set Up	Posture Reset	Lean from the ankles	Lean from the ankles	Lean from the ankles
1	Baby Step Jog in place 5×(1 min. on/1 min. off) 2–3x/day	Baby Step Jog with Strap/Lean 5×(1 min. on/1 min. off) 2–3x/day	Lean/Fall + Small Step Contrast Run @ 180spm 3–4×100m with contrast lean every 20m	Full Step Run @ 180spm+ 2–3×(100m in 26 sec. w/ 2 min. recovery) = 7:00 min. pace
2	BSJ in place 1×(1 min. on/1 min. off) 2×(2 min. on/1 min. off) 2–3x/day	BSJ with Strap/Lean 1×(1 min. on/1 min. off) 2×(2 min. on/1 min. off) 2–3x/day	REST	REST
3	BSJ in place @ 180spm 1×(1 min. on/1 min. off) 2×(2 min. on/1 min. off) 2–3x/day	BSJ with Strap/Lean @ 180spm 1×(1 min. on/1 min. off) 2×(2 min. on/1 min. off) 2–3x/day	Lean/Fall + Medium Step Contrast Run @ 180spm 3–4×100m with contrast lean every 25m	Full Step Run @ 180spm+ 2–3×(100m in 22 sec. w/ 2 min. recovery) = 6:00 min. pace
4	BSJ in place @ 180spm 1×(2 min. on/1 min. off) 1×(3 min. on/1 min. off) 2–3x/day	BSJ with Strap/Lean @ 180spm 1×(2 min. on/1 min. off) 1×(3 min. on/1 min. off) 2–3x/day	REST	REST
5	BSJ in place @ 180spm 1×(5 min. on/1 min. off) 2–3x/day	BSJ with Strap/Lean @ 180spm 1×(5 min. on/1 min. off) 2–3x/day	Lean/Fall + Full Step Contrast Run @ 190spm 3–4×100m with contrast lean every 30m	Full Step Run @ 180spm+ 2–3×(100m in 20 sec. w/ 2 min. recovery) = 5:20 min. pace
6	Repeat Day 5 - Optional	Repeat Day 5 - Optional	REST	REST
7	REST	REST	REST	REST
Skill	Proper landing	Proper landing with modest lean	Proper landing/ lean/fwd. motion	Running with good form
Total Steps	4,000–10,000 steps/week	4,000–10,000 steps/ week		

Courtesy of Walt Reynolds, NovaSport Athlete Development.

After proper running form is established, form drills should continue several times per week throughout the duration of the overall program. Regular video work should be undertaken roughly once every couple of weeks to ensure that a runner does not revert back to prior, bad habits in running form.

Points About Form Training

Several concepts need to be kept in mind when a runner embarks on a period of form training.

Do You Fling, Drop, Stop, and Flop?

For the vast majority of runners, four key words describe form: fling, drop, stop, and flop. Most runners fling a leg forward prior to impact with the ground, and it is usually a relatively straight leg that is flung forward (figure 15.1*a*). They then drop the foot of the forward leg directly downward instead of sweeping it backward, thus creating a large SAT and a major braking force (figure 15.1*b*). As the heel of the foot hits the ground, it stops

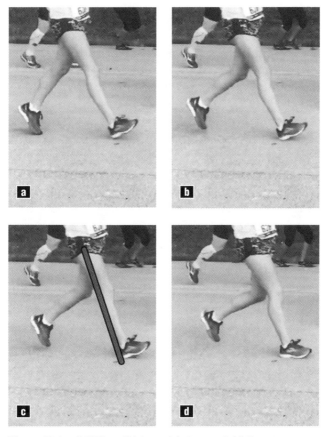

Figure 15.1 *(a)* Fling, *(b)* drop, *(c)* stop, and *(d)* flop.

forward movement and permits major shock forces to travel quickly up the leg into the hip (figure 15.1c). Then, the sole of the foot flops onto the ground (figure 15.1d).

Putting some numbers on this pattern of fling, drop, stop, and flop, for most runners the leg flings out to an MSA of about 18 degrees during moderate-intensity running. The drop of the foot without backward sweep then produces an SAT of about 16 degrees. The stop and flop ensure that forces equal to one times body weight and 1.5 times body weight are reached before the shin even reaches a vertical position. In other words, high vertical propulsive forces are produced before the leg and body are in the proper position for forward movement. In addition, with fling, drop, stop, and flop, VALR is maximized (VALR is the rate of loading of impact force in the leg after impact, which is the best predictor of running injury; as VALR increases, injury risk rises).

Or Swing, Sweep, Coil, and Spring?

In contrast with the fling, drop, stop, and flop pattern, the distance runner with good form uses a strategy of swing, sweep, coil, and spring. With a flexed knee, she swings her leg forward under control and achieves an MSA of about 14 degrees (figure 15.2a). Instead of dropping her foot to the ground, she then sweeps her foot backward to achieve an SAT of about six degrees (and thus a fairly nice ROS/MSA ratio of 8/14, or .57) (figure 15.2b). She then makes contact with the ground with her midfoot; her foot, ankle, and leg coil elastically into a dynamic, spring-like appendage that is ready to thrust the body upward and forward with high force (figure 15.2c). Finally, she springs upward and forward, producing vertical and horizontal propulsive forces at exactly the right time (figure 15.2d). This pattern is what may be called the "holy grail" of running form.

Beware of Those Shoes

Companies and retail outlets that sell running shoes have made a major effort to convince runners that certain models of shoes enhance form by controlling pronation and "improving stability." The truth is that the modern shoe corrupts form by encouraging heel-striking—a result of the foamy, built-up heels featured in so many shoes. The ancillary truths are that pronation (traditionally viewed as an injury producing ankle action) is actually a natural part of the gait cycle and is not an injury-producing evil. Running shoes with thick "protective" midsoles, far from encouraging stability, actually increase instability and thus promote injury.

Good running form is the result of proper positioning of the legs and feet; it is not optimized by the purchase of particular brands and models of

Figure 15.2   *(a)* Swing, *(b)* sweep, *(c)* coil, and *(d)* spring.

running shoes. Such proper positioning of the legs and feet is the result of relentless form drilling rather than favorable lacing. In fact, great form can be established in any running shoes; the purchase of a specific type of shoes is not necessary for terrific form.

A Quick-Start Guide

If the various form drills and techniques that provide a pathway to the holy grail of form seem daunting, bear in mind that a runner can develop an initial feeling for proper foot position and optimal SAT using a kind of "quick-start guide" as follows.

1. Kick off your shoes and socks and begin running at moderate pace with small steps, making sure that you feel the middle portion of each foot making the initial contact with the ground and the heel hitting earth a few milliseconds after the midfoot.

2. Deliberately run for 20 meters or so on your heels. Notice how awful this feels!

3. Return to midfoot-striking and practice running with relatively small step lengths for one minute, making certain that you are landing with the midfoot, rather than the heel.

4. Take a short break and then repeat the pattern for another minute, really relaxing and feeling what you are doing.

5. Repeat three more times.

Some runners are able to improve their form employing only this quick-start guide.

Always remember, too, that there are no more than three rules of good form, which a runner should keep in mind when completing the form training outlined in this book:

1. You must swing your foot and leg forward.

2. You must sweep your leg and foot backward to make strong contact with the ground with the midfoot, just a little ahead of your body.

3. You must push hard on the ground with the foot, propelling your body upward and forward.

Conclusion

There is no getting around it: Distance running is a contact sport that involves 170 to 200 collisions of a runner's body with the ground per minute. Each contact with the ground can produce a ground-reaction force of two to five times body weight, which in turn can produce either a high running velocity—or great risk of injury. The forces created when a foot hits the ground are either your velocity booster or your "breaking and braking" enemy. To run with good form, you must handle the unavoidable impact forces in an optimal manner. You can manage them in ways that prevent injury and upgrade speed, or in a manner which slows you down and gets you hurt. May the forces be with you!

References

1. O. Anderson, *Running Science* (Champaign, IL: Human Kinetics, 2014), 449–451.
2. Ibid.

Index

About the Author

Owen Anderson

Owen Anderson, PhD, is the coach and manager of some of the best runners in the world, including Cynthia Limo (silver medalist in the 2016 IAAF World Half Marathon Championship and first-ranked road racer in the world according to ARRS in 2016), Mary Wacera (world silver and bronze medalist in the 2014 and 2016 IAAF World Half Marathons), Monicah Ngige (two-time winner of the Cooper River Bridge Run 10K and champion of the 2017 Monterey Bay Half Marathon), Mary Wangui (victor at the 2017 Tulsa Run 15K), Iveen Chepkemoi (first in the 2017 AK Sotik Cross Country meeting in Kenya), and Gladys Kipsoi (winner of the 2017 Pittsburgh Half Marathon).

Owen is the author of five books on running: Lactate Lift-Off, Great Workouts for Popular Races, Aurora, Running Science, and Running Form. He has written hundreds of articles on running for publications such as National Geographic Adventure, Runner's World, Shape, Men's Health, Peak Performance, Sports Injury Bulletin, and Running Research News.

Owen has been a featured speaker at symposiums around the world, including seminars at City University, London; Osaka University; and the University of Tokyo. Owen, who speaks Swahili fluently, has traveled to Kenya on 25 different occasions to manage running camps, recruit elite athletes, and study the training habits and nutritional practices of elite Kenyan runners. During the summer, he hosts running camps throughout the United States.

In his free time, Owen enjoys helping kids. He assisted in rescuing Kenyan children from the Tana Delta region during the savage conflicts of 2013 and has helped these young people resume their academic pursuits.